Frances Langford
Armed Forces
Sweetheart

Frances Langford
Armed Forces Sweetheart

by Ben Ohmart

BearManor Media

2018

Frances Langford: Armed Forces Sweetheart

Published in the United States of America by:

BearManor Media
P. O. Box 71426
Albany, GA 31708

BearManorMedia.com

Printed in the United States.

Typesetting and layout by John Teehan

ISBN—978-1-62933-213-0

For Emily

Table of Contents

Introduction 1

1. Humble Beginnings 3

2. Hollywood 33

3. Bob Hope 73

4. Hollywood Stop 121

5. "I'll Kiss You Goodnight In the Morning" 161

6. Bye, Bye, Hollywood 183

7. A New Love 193

8. Hand Still In 207

9. The Later Years 213

    Appendix 1 227
        Letters

    Appendix 2 233
        Selected Purple Heart Diary Columns

    Appendix 3 261
        Frances Langford Radio Credits

    Appendix 4 281
        Frances Langford Credits & Sources

Index 329

Introduction

I HAVE TO ADMIT, for years and years, all I knew about Frances Langford came from The Bickersons, my *favorite* radio show. It wasn't really a radio series, except briefly, when Frances and Lew Parker did it for a weekly 30 minutes. Before that, it was a series of veniettes and highly successful albums that caused me enough guffaws to cause me to track down the son of creator Philip Rapp years later and request to write a book on the Bickersons.

One of the first things I did was call Frances Langford. Paul Rapp, son of Phil, gave me her phone number. It was my trek into speaking with royalty. For royalty supreme, she was. She was gracious, friendly, sincerely cared to hear from me and to know my thoughts, and above all, helpful.

Many people helped me with this book, so a big Thank You to Shirley Lee Ames, Randy Bonneville, Celia Langford Chirstensen, Stephan Eichenberg, Sandra Grabman, Martin Grams, Jr., Walden Hughes, Sidney M Markowitz, David Menefee, Walt Mitchell, Tony Romano, Bret Roy (SgtMaj USMC Ret.), Derek Teague, Charles Tranberg, Chris Valenti, and Laura Wagner.

Special thanks to The Martin County Historical Society/The Elliott Museum for letting me have access to the thousands of photos and articles that make up the Frances Langford Collection. It is an amazing sight to behold. And many thanks to Evans Crary, Jr., Trustee of the Estate for making that possible.

While not all photos in this book could be identified, I did not want to leave them out just because of that. Obviously, Frances cared a lot about her war work, and more than anything, I wanted this book to showcase her *amazing* patriotism.

Thank you, Frances.

– Ben Ohmart
May 2017

1 Humble Beginnings

CELIA LANGFORD CHIRSTENSEN, author of several Langford family history books, writes:

The Name – "Langford" or "Lankford"?

The two names (plus "Lanceford" and "Longford") have been used interchangeably in America for over 300 years. Historians say that the name originated in ancient Britain to designate the residents of a placed called "the long ford." Over generations many variations have been used. The names were not spelled consistently because many, or most, of the emigrants could not read or write and could not supply a proper spelling. Neither could most of the settlers who were already here. They recorded the names as they sounded in many cases. Often both Lankford and Langford are used in the same court record, and sometimes in the same paragraph!

When our ancestor, John, was in Georgia his name was recorded as "Lankford" but when he moved to Florida, he used the Langford spelling. Naturally, we feel "Langford" is the correct spelling, but there are probably Lankford cousins who are just as convinced theirs is the "true" spelling.

Our Langfords probably came from England, and most likely arrived in Virginia. There are Langfords recorded in Virginia by 1638. I suspect our Langfords arrived in Virginia in the 1600s, then moved down into North Carolina. I believe our John came from North Carolina to Georgia after the Revolutionary War. There are several other Langfords (Jesse, Moses, and Parish) who were listed with John in the taxpayer list of Granville County, North Carolina in 1784. Jesse, Moses,

Parish and John all seem to have moved down to Wilkes and then Tattnall Co., Georgia about the same time – indicating a likely relationship (probably all brothers as they were of a similar age).

Born Frances Newbern Langford in Lakeland, Florida on April 4, 1913 to a carpenter (or possibly a building contractor) and his wife Anna Rhea Newbern, a concert pianist, Frances was already drawn to the outdoors, especially when it came to fishing. "All we did for fun back then was camping and fishing," she said. "I loved it then and I still love it."

After Lakeland High, she took a year at Florida Southern College. But got sidetracked by a career.

"I started out just singing by myself," Frances explained. "Then I began to wonder if I could sing in front of people – and would they like me." She was studying music at college when she had to go into the hospital for a complicated tonsillectomy. She had had a lovely soprano voice, but after the operation she found it had dropped to a contralto. And also then discovered she was singing better than ever. One sensational press release claims that the doctor's hand slipped during the operation and his knife cut too far, changing forever her dream of becoming an operatic soprano. "I look at it as everything happens for the best," she said. "An operatic career would have cost lots of money. Instead, I began singing blues songs with my new deep voice and was suddenly a big hit in school.

"My mother was a great influence in my life—encouraging me in every way. She was a concert pianist and played all the time. I washed the dishes and did anything else that needed to be done around the house just to get her to play for us."

Frances started singing at local Lions Clubs and other local venues. Her first professional gig was singing on a weekly program for WDAE or WFLA for $5 a week at the age of 15. It was sponsored by Tampa cigar magnate Eli Whitt. "My dad said, 'The gasoline costs that much to go there and back,' and my mother said, 'Well, maybe someday she can pay you back.' I think I did."

In 1930, a Tampa, Florida radio station director heard her sing at an American Legion party and hired her. A year later, Frances' mother drove her down to Miami, where Rudy Vallee was performing. He came bouncing into the room with his shirttails out and said he'd listen to the girl. She only got through 16 bars of a song when he stopped her and said, "That's enough. My secretary will call you and tell you when to come to

New Orleans." Frances recalled: "It was my first trip out of the state. I was thrilled to death." He picked her for a guest spot for his radio show, her debut on nationwide radio. That led to her first radio series in New York in 1931.

Another version of her big break was reported thusly: after winning first prize in a singing contest, she attracted the eye of bandleader Eli Witt. Witt's friend, Rudy Vallee, had announced that he would be picking his guest star next week in Florida. Witt called Vallee in Miami and asked him to listen in to his program to find his "find." Rudy did, and immediately asked Witt to send her down to the Olympia Theatre in Miami. Frances sang a few numbers for him backstage.

Regardless of how her big break happened, Vallee *was* instrumental in getting her on NBC, personally taking her to WOR in New York City, where she was signed for a year. "I was doing commercial shows, and all of a sudden I was making money."

By November 1931 she was on Broadway in Peter Arno's *Here Goes the Bride*, which opened on November 3rd and closed on November 7th, for a total of seven performances. She also appeared in *The Pure in Heart* on Broadway at the Longacre Theatre. It was a play in four scenes which opened on March 20, 1934 and lasted a total of seven performances.

One night that same year in New York, Frances sang "Night and Day" at a party at the Waldorf-Astoria honoring Cole Porter. It's said that Paramount producer Walter Wanger was at that party and was so impressed with the young lady that he asked her to Hollywood for a screen test. Other reports state he signed her up *without* a screen test. When Frances began appearing on *Hollywood Hotel*, Louella Parsons' radio show, hosted by Dick Powell, while out West, she also appeared in the movie version of the series.

When Frances returned home to Lakeland (for a vacation), the local press made a big to do about their local-girl-makes-good who was to appear at the Polk Theatre for three shows on June 5, 1934. By then Frances had performed a myriad of nightclub, radio (sometimes three shows a week) and vaudeville dates. Lakeland was (and continues to be) impressed.

Ed Sullivan himself, in his *New York News* column, wrote in 1934, "The No. 1 singer among the youngsters, Frances Langford, this column's protégé." She appeared at the Simplon Club on West 53rd St., managed by her big brother Jimmy. It was on opening night at the Simplon that Frances caught the eye of critic/raconteur George Jean Nathan, and soon the couple were in the gossip columns together. Because of him (early news stories state), Frances took dramatic lessons which led to screen tests with Paramount, Fox, Warner Bros. and RKO. The Nathan relationship must not have been serious, for when Frances was asked at the time what sort of man she was looking for, she stated, "If I could meet a boy from out of town, as innocent and scared of New York as I am; if I knew I could love him—I'd give up my career, success, and all that goes with it. But I doubt if I ever will. That kind of man is afraid of me. They read the papers, see me on the stage, and think I'm some man-eating vampire. Really, I want a home and kids more than all the newspaper headlines in the world."

When the Empire State Building was dedicated, Frances was on hand to be photographed with ex-Governor Langford of New York. She then appeared in some Warner short subjects, shot in Astoria, New York, which Frances (at the time) said "were awful."

She was busy mostly with radio and nightclub dates, but was going to give up the nightclub circuit to take on another radio series, *The Studebaker Program*, on CBS. She also had radio contracts for *Colgate House Party*, *Richard Himber* and *Plough's Musical Courier*. She was already set to appear in New York's *George White's Scandals* and *Radio City Revels*. She kept busy, and with lots of publicity, too. One article caught her "Relaxing" on the roof garden of her New York apartment with handfuls of cats, showing the petite brunette "just fooling around" with Blackie and Goldie when not busy with NBC shows. She mentioned that she would send for her pet raccoon from Lakeland soon. Her present contract stated that she could not leave New York until the first of the year, at which point the plan was to go conquer Hollywood.

Some early glamour shots of Frances.

"Frances Langford beams from the car door of her new yellow Cord, a new acquisition which made her holidays a gala time for her. The photo was taken at her home in Lakeland, FL, where she recently spent a month's vacation."

Frances, the brunette years.

January 1936 publicity shot.

Left to right: Buddy Ebsen, Frances Langford, Virginia Bruce, James Stewart, Eleanor Powell, Sid Silvers and Una Merkel in a CBS radio broadcast of *Born to Dance* (1936 MGM musical).

"Bicycling's great sport for Frances Langford, diminutive singer on *Hollywood Hotel* and featured in the currently showing, *Born to Dance*, MGM picture. Frances has just returned to California from a month's vacation in her hometown, Lakeland, FL."

Frances in Florida.

Dancing with University of Florida football captain, Bill Chase.

More early publicity stills.

"Frances Langford and Jerry Cooper, popular radio favorites of *Hollywood Hotel*, get together for a duet."

Frances on stage.

Relaxing in Sewall's Point, Florida.

1936 publicity still for a Walter Wanger production.

644-226

Some early photos.

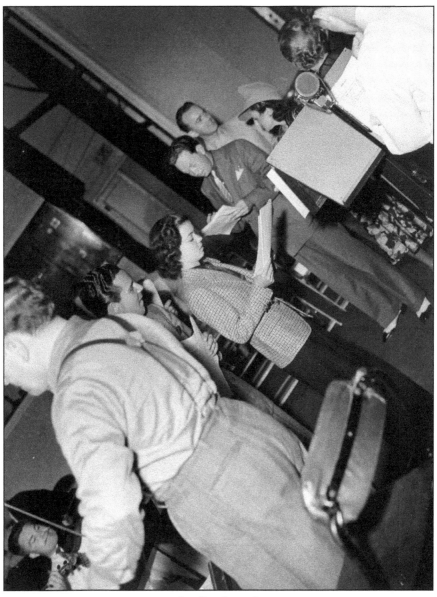

A radio rehearsal.

2 Hollywood

FRANCES LANGFORD'S FILM DEBUT was *Every Night at Eight* (1935) for Paramount. *Variety* said she "gives promise of going places." This was the movie that contained what would be her signature tune for the rest of her career: "I'm in the Mood for Love." She also co-authored two of the film's songs, "Then You've Never Been Blue," and "Speaking Confidentially." The score was such an immediate hit, she recorded four songs in July of that same year with Mahlon Merrick's orchestra for Brunswick Records.

Frances played Susan Moore who, along with Dixie Foley (Alice Faye) and Daphne OConnor (Patsy Kelly), are fired from their Huxley's Mint Julep Company job when their boss discovers them making a record on company time. Bandleader "Tops" Cardona (George Raft) makes the trio a singing sensation under the name "the Swanee Sisters," though they are not from the South.

Hopping over to MGM, Frances joined Jack Benny, Eleanor Powell, Robert Taylor and others in *Broadway Melody of 1936* (1935), a delightful musical romp with some classic songs from Nacio Herb Brown and Arthur Freed. Frances played "herself" to sing "You Are My Lucky Star" and "Broadway Rhythm." The backstage Broadway musical plot contained lots of snappy tap dancing from Eleanor Powell, and was the screen debut of Buddy Ebsen and his sister Vilma. The film was nominated for a Best Picture Oscar, and Moss Hart's original story received an Oscar nod as well. Dave Gould won an Oscar for dance direction. The film was one of the biggest hits of 1935.

Frances ran back and forth between Paramount and MGM. Back at home/Paramount, she appeared in the Joe Penner vehicle, *Collegiate* (1936), based on the novel and play by Alice Duer Miller. Frances portrays Juliet Hay, the very proper secretary at an unsuccessful girl's school which

Jerry Craig (Penner) has inherited from his aunt. It's a breezy 9-reel musical in which Frances sings Mack Gordon/Harry Revel's "You Hit the Spot" and gets her playboy of a man at the end. *Variety* stated that it was "fair entertainment. Light, diverting, no sock, but no bore."

Cole Porter's first original movie musical, *Born to Dance* (1936), was another sailors-in-New-York musical comedy and contained one of his greatest standards, "I've Got You Under My Skin," sung by Virginia Bruce in the film. But Frances made it a hit thanks to her Decca record contract. In the movie, Frances was Peppy Turner, singing "Swinging the Jinx Away," also used years later in *I Dood It!* by Red Skelton. "Easy to Love," one of Porter's best ballads, was pleasantly sung by star James Stewart. *Variety* thought it "corking entertainment."

Next it was off to Republic Pictures in 1937 for *The Hit Parade* (1937) with Phil Regan and the Duke Ellington and Eddy Duchin orchestras. Frances Langford "as the warbling ingénue looks good as photographed and plows into her numbers with authority," wrote *Variety*. She appears as Ruth Allison, a young singer who makes it big in radio, despite her having been in prison on a trumped up charge, and wins the governor's pardon and the man (Phil Regan) she loves. It was an expensive film: a budget of $500,000, Republic's most expensive film to date.

This was followed by the film version of her popular radio series, *Hollywood Hotel* (1937), directed by Busby Berkeley. It's a musical love story about a singer (Dick Powell) and star Mona Marshall (Lola Lane) at the Hollywood Hotel, a real gathering place for movie people, but which had lost its star-pulling power before it was shot. Backed by Benny Goodman, Frances sang "Let That Be a Lesson to You," and dueted with Jerry Cooper on "Silhouetted in the Moonlight." Louella Parsons, host of the radio series, made her screen debut in this movie. Both Campbell Soup, sponsor of the series, and the owners of the hotel sued Warner Bros. for using the title without permission.

Frances is listed as a cast member in the production charts for United Artists' *Walter Wanger's Vogues of 1938* (1937), but it's difficult to confirm if her participation in the Technicolor musical comedy starring Warner Baxter and Joan Bennett is true.

Gossip reports stated at the time that she had been "going with" George Jean Nathan, Gary Cooper, Walter Winchell and Frank Parker during her time in Hollywood. This is around the time she met Jon Hall, whom she called "the handsomest man ever to come out of Hollywood." They were married in Arizona on June 4, 1938.

Jon Hall was born Charles Felix Locher, on February 23, 1915 en route to San Francisco by train when they made an emergency stop in Fresno, California, so he could be born. His Swiss-born father, Felix Locher (pronounced Lo-Shay), was a figure skating champion and inventor, and later became a character actor in movies. The Lochers raised their son in Tahiti, later publicity claiming that Jon's maternal grandmother was once the queen of Tahiti.

Growing up, Jon's developed swimming and diving skills, both of which would come in handy in Hollywood. He briefly studied engineering, languages, and science at International University in Geneva, Switzerland, and at England's Badingham College. After the family moved to Los Angeles, 20-year-old Hall made his film debut in a small part in Monogram's *Women Must Dress* (1935). When 20th Century-Fox signed him, he started making movies under the name Charles Locher. He had the juvenile lead in *Charlie Chan in Shanghai* (1935), but the studio did little else for him.

One of Jon's best roles during this time came as the title character in the low-budget indie, *The Lion Man* (1935). When he later became a star, this movie would be re-released to capitalize on his fame. In two 1937 movies, *Mind Your Own Business* and *The Girl from Scotland Yard*, he was billed as Lloyd Crane. He also unsuccessfully tested for the role of Flash Gordon at Universal.

His uncle, James Norman Hall, co-author of the novels *Mutiny on the Bounty* and *The Hurricane*, helped him get his big break. In 1937, Jon was visiting his uncle at Goldwyn Studios, where the screen version of *The Hurricane* was scheduled to start shooting. The big-budget movie was to star Dorothy Lamour, but they were still without a leading man. Several actors were tested but proved unsuitable and Joel McCrea had turned the assignment down. The moment director John Ford saw the 6'2", 195-pound handsome Charles Locher, he knew he had found his star–plus, he could do most of his own swimming.

Renamed Jon Hall, he became a star overnight with his casting in *The Hurricane* (1937). "Goldwyn's Gift to Women" was everywhere in the press. Unfortunately, Sam Goldwyn did not strike while his star was hot and he did not put him in another movie. Other producers wanted to borrow Hall, notably Alexander Korda who sought to star Hall in his colorful spectacle *The Thief of Bagdad*, but Goldwyn rejected all offers.

There were some indications that along with being handsome, Jon was something of a hothead. The few newspaper reports that appeared about him weren't positive. On November 31, 1944 he was in Los Angeles Superior Court, telling a jury how he was "beat up pretty badly" and almost killed by band leader Tommy Dorsey. Hall stated it wasn't he who paid "undue attention" to Dorsey's wife, actress Pat Dane, but another actor, Eddie Norris, last August 5th. But Hall got the whooping with a knife (perhaps by Dane or a man named "Smiley") which took 50 stitches to close. He had put his arm around the wife in question, and when Dorsey protested, Hall accused him of "smoking the wrong kind of cigarettes." Hall's nose was also busted, for which he took an "acid treatment to get it looking right again." The left nostril had been sliced through but the surgery left a scar, for which the acid was supposed to erase the scar. The fight took place at 2 a.m. at the Clover Club (though Jon stated it all happened in Dorsey's apartment). Frances was at the time on tour in the South Pacific. The trial continued for several days.

Soon after their marriage, Mr. and Mrs. Hall took a jaunt to Central Florida, then called the Treasure Coast. "We were just riding around from one beach to another," she said, "and then we got to Jensen Beach and we happened to see this driveway that rose up. We drove in, thinking the whole time, 'Gee, this is not what you're supposed to do.'" They fell in love with the place. "These people came out of the house, and the first words out of our mouths were, 'Is your place for sale?'" It wasn't, but the offer made the house owners think twice, and soon Jon and Frances had a home with more than 100 acres for $15,000. Frances could afford it. She was making over $2,000 a week by now; $1500 for *Hollywood Hotel*, and $750 from MGM.

"It those days, Jensen Beach wasn't as big as Lakeland," Frances explained. "Lakeland had beautiful lakes, this had beautiful rivers. And you could have all the property in the world that you wanted, and nobody was next door. We had the highest spot around here—at least 50 feet above sea level!"

Because of their developmental plans with the area, they were given the singular honor of being elected Honorary President of the Jensen Beach Auxiliary Business Men's Association—for life. They were already co-owners (with Robert Young) of the Cloverleaf Aviation Corp. in Hollywood. Jon had designed the Cloverleaf Hanger. One of his Cloverleafs was set to be erected at the Stuart Airport in Florida—a four-plane hangar. They were planning a development of Langford-Hall Estates, including a nightclub called *Jon*, one called *The Beachcombers*, a hotel and cottages—all in the Jensen Beach area. Jon would bring his collection of Tahitian and Samoan art treasures to give the clubs and hotel "an authentic South Sea atmosphere." They were also later slated to star together in a series of six western pictures for 20th Century-Fox, to begin in Nevada in June of 1949.

FRANCES' RECORDING CAREER began in 1931 when Victor Records signed her up, but didn't release her recordings. Then the Columbia Phonograph Company grabbed Frances in August of 1932 to croon out tunes like "I Can't Believe It's True" and "Having a Good Time, Wish You Were Here." In 1935 she signed with Decca Records. One of her first songs released from them was the song she sang in *Palm Springs* (1936), "I Don't Want to Make History." She stayed with the label until 1942, performing with the best: Jimmy Dorsey, Victor Young, Harry Sosnick and others.

Palm Springs was a Paramount picture based on Myles Connolly's short story, "Lady Smith," which appeared in *Good Housekeeping* magazine that same year. For a change, Frances is the true star and focus in the plot, which tells the story of a rich girl who is suddenly poor and finds herself on make for a rich husband, and finds one in a cowboy by the name of Slim (Smith Ballew). It was the first screen role for Smith, radio emcee, singer and orchestra leader.

Taking a few years off from pictures to belt out a lot of records, Frances also did a fair amount of radio work. She appeared on *The Texaco Star Theatre* for CBS during 1939 and 1940. It co-starred Ken Murray and Kenny Baker.

1940 saw Frances back on celluloid in Lum and Abner's debut picture, *Dreaming Out Loud* for RKO. She played Alice, who worked at the post office, and was having trouble getting married to Kenneth Barnes (Robert Wilcox) because of her selfish aunt (Clara Blandick). There was only one song in the film, the title song. *Money Isn't Everything* was its working title, and it was the first of six Lum and Abner films.

Too Many Girls (1940) nearly gave Lucille Ball a chance to sing, though her songs were dubbed. The RKO picture, based on the Rodgers & Hart musical produced on Broadway the preceding year, boasting the hit "I Didn't Know What Time It Was," was a fun college musical also starring Ann Miller, Eddie Bracken, Desi Arnaz and Frances as one of the college girls. Lucy and Desi met during the filming of this movie and married the following year.

The Hit Parade of 1941 (1940) let Frances and Kenny Baker share the leads of a small radio station trying to stay afloat with their main advertiser (a junk shop). They had a lovely duet of "Who Am I?" (nominated for an Oscar), while Frances sang "Swing Low, Sweet Rhythm" later as a solo. It was intended to be a straight follow-up to *Hit Parade*, but the film kept getting delayed.

Hollywood was blonde, and so were the popular Alice Faye and Betty Grable. And now, in *All-American Co-Ed* (1941), so was Frances Langford in this Hal Roach/United Artists college musical. She remained a blonde.

Swing It Soldier shot for about a week in mid-May and was released on July 11, 1941 for Universal. This romantic comedy with songs puts Frances in the role of twins, one pregnant with a soldier-husband, and the other falling for draftee Jerry Trainor (Ken Murray) who, naturally, thinks one singer twin is the other. As the alternate/working title of the film, *Radio Revels of 1942*, suggests, there were many radio performers involved in the radio plot, including Don Wilson of the *Jack Benny Program*, and Hanley Stafford who had finally escaped *Baby Snooks*.

"Mrs. Frieda Locher, Mother of Jon Hall, lunches at the same table with Mrs. Langford, mother of Frances Langford, wife of Jon Hall. The luncheon was held at the Brown Derby in Hollywood, providing a good opportunity for the various mothers to discuss their talented movie star children with people who understand their problems."

"Jon Hall and his beautiful wife, Frances Langford demonstrate the easy and perfectly proper Hawaiian mode of eating at the Luau given by them for friends in their Westwood home."

Patsy Kelly, Alice Faye, and Frances in *Every Night at Eight*, 1935.

Mr. and Mrs. Jon Hall apparently have the dance floor to themselves in the Palm Room of the Beverly Hills Hotel.

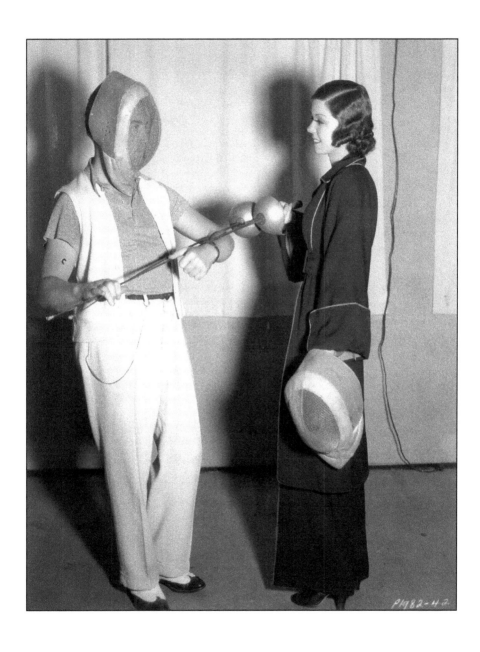

Broadway Melody of 1936
(1935).

Palm Springs (1936).

Palm Springs (1936).

Palm Springs (1936).

Palm Springs (1936).

Receiving the *Radio Guide* Award of 1937.

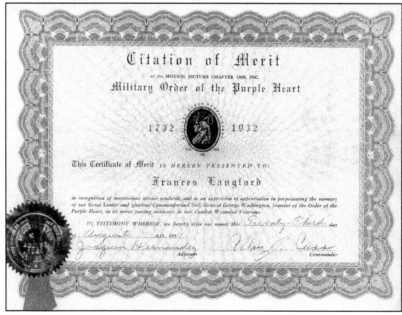

MEMBERSHIP LIST

published by

THE OFFICAL FRANCES LANGFORD FAN CLUB

FEDERATION   1940

HONORARY PRESIDENT   ACTIVE PRESIDENT

Frances Langford   Eddie M Lally

HONORARY VICE PRESIDENT   HONORARY SECRETARY

Jon Hall   Louise Locher

INTERNATIONAL SECRETARY   CHAPTER HEAD

Bertha Quintana   Cecile Morris

ASSISTANT CHAPTER HEAD   EDITOR

Polly Ashemore   Eddie M Lally

CHAPTER LEADERS

WISCONSIN   ENGLAND

Ruth Cantwell   Geoffrey Pritchard

TEXAS   SCOTLAND

Cecile Morris   Weymess Craigie

HOLLYWOOD   INDIA

Blanche Livingston   Noreen Foscholo

-.-.-.-.-

Frances Langford

Lucille Ball and Frances in *Too Many Girls* (1940).

At Clover Leaf Aviation with husband Jon.

Frances and husband Jon Hall scouting Jensen Beach, FL.

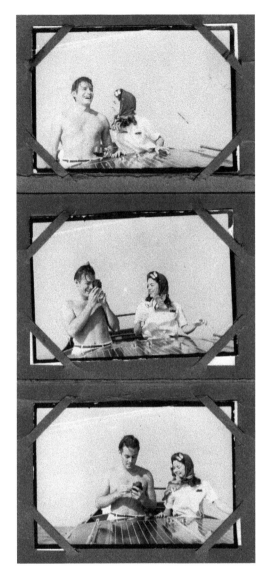

Swing It Soldier, AKA *Radio Revels of 1942,* with Skinnay Ennis.

Too Many Girls (1940).

3

Bob Hope

FRANCES WAS DOING A LOT of radio in 1941. She was heard on *American Cruise* with frequent radio co-star Dick Powell. She was also heard on one of Bob Hope's radio shows for Pepsodent in 1941 (possibly replacing Judy Garland). It was apparently Bob's first military program, broadcast from March Field in Riverside, California. And the response was so positive, Bob started playing for more training bases. He asked Frances to join him. "We hopped all over the United States for two seasons," she said. "I really wanted to do something worthwhile for my country. Everywhere I went, it was the same thing. I got up and sang about eight bars of 'I'm in the Mood for Love' and way in the back some GI would stand up. He'd say, 'You've come to the right place, sister!' They responded to everything, they were such a wonderful audience."

Tony Romano, Jerry Colonna, Bob Hope and Frances Langford comprised the group known as Bob Hope's Four Gypsies. "We were just a foursome that clicked," Romano said. "There was a great rapport between the four of us. We did shows on the backs of trucks. We did shows in fields. Right after that, we would get on the plane and go to the next show. It was hit-and-run. We traveled over 11 million miles. We saw millions of GIs.

"I believe the communication Frances had with these audiences was the great love and feeling that every guy out there was just like her brother. I feel that was a very big thing. So when she walked out, there was a great communication even before she sang.

"She's a singer who tells the greatest story. Everything she believes in she tells you. So you're not just listening to a singer, you're listening to a storyteller. That is hard to find.

"There was one trip to the South Pacific. We were on a seaplane that ferried us from New Caledonia to Australia and we had to make a forced landing on the ocean. Bob came up to me and said, 'Tony you're a singer, you must have good ears. Do you hear anything odd?' I told him no. Then just minutes later, we found out that both of the engines were dead. The next thing we knew, the pilot was telling us to jettison everything.

"We gathered up Frances's wardrobe and the plane tools and several cases of cigarettes and a case of scotch we were taking to the soldiers. The tools went first, followed by the clothes, then the cigarettes. We finally got to the case of scotch. Jerry Colonna handed it to me and said to throw it so it hits on a corner and doesn't break the bottles.

"After circling a while, the plane hit the water, then bounced up about 50 feet before it rested on a sandbar. The plane was just sitting there. A whole bunch of boats full of civilians came up to us and took us the last 30 miles to Australia. They'd been watching our plane circling, circling, they knew we were in trouble.

"Sometimes the lodgings were as tough to deal with as the transport. Sometimes the four of us slept on the ground in those pup tents, just like the soldiers did. I remember one night, it was in Europe. I felt something on my stomach. I asked Bob what he was doing, but he didn't say anything. A few minutes later, something patted me on the tummy. I had a flashlight and I turned it on. There were four kangaroo rats about two feet long there! I told the GIs the next morning, and they said, 'Those are our pets.'

"But, the tours weren't as rough as you might think. We had youth on our side. I was 26 when we started. We never thought it would be a lot of work. We had so much fun traveling, seeing places we'd never seen.

"After the war, the four of us still performed together for the troops overseas, along with shows at the White House. But the USO shows stand out because the soldiers always appreciated what we did the most. It gave us a good feeling. All those guys smiling. It was unforgettable."

In Sicily, the troupe eventually met General Patton, but it took some doing. "His aide at the time," recalled Romano, "told us he was too busy and kind of fluffed us off. So we went ahead with plans for the show and a spaghetti dinner I was going to cook. Just before the show, the aide appeared and said Patton would like to see Hope now. 'Are you kidding?' Hope said. 'We're booked. We're having Romano spaghetti. We tried to see him this afternoon.' The aide actually turned pale and started pleading with us. 'I can't go back and tell him you won't come. Please, Mr. Hope. It will only take an hour.' 'My first joke takes more than an hour,'

Hope said. That aide stayed through the show and kept pleading, so we did go, finally.

"Patton wanted to know all about the show and we ended up doing the whole thing for him. He was so interesting, we stayed there until early morning. He told us this description of war being like a football game. 'You gain 10 yards,' he said, 'you lose 5, but you're always striving for the touchdown. But if I see where the goal is, you better believe I'm going to get there.'"

When they had dinner with the General, Frances was warned about this tough man. But after dinner, Patton read a letter he had written about his longtime aide who had been killed just a few days earlier. He started to cry. "That," she said, "was a wonderful man."

In Tunisia, they performed for a mobile hospital that just did not want them to leave. But when dusk came, they were warned that German fighter planes were coming. Speeding across the desert, the troupe jumped into a ditch, Frances jumping right on top of Bob. Hope said, "Oh, I'm hit!" To which Frances replied in her best Blanche Bickerson, "You're not hit, get up from there!"

"She knows just how much sex to pour and still be dignified," Bob Hope said. Often, he would introduce Frances with the line, "Boys… this is what you're fighting for…" as she took the stage.

"She was not a sex symbol like others were," Romano said. "She never pushed that or even thought about it. She was just their pal and buddy, but the feminine came through, all right. In fact, when she'd walk on stage they'd start screaming and hollering right away."

Frances said of Bob, "He was the best in the world. He was always happy. He entertained us. His heart was in it."

While doing a monologue for the troops stationed at Camp Roberts in central California, Bob Hope did a string of jokes about the bus ride to get there. At one point he quipped, "The bus went through a dark tunnel and, just as a gag, I leaned over to steal a kiss from Frances Langford. Just then, the bus hit a bump! Well, all I can say is that either I kissed the saxophone player or Frances should stop smokin' White Owls!"

FRANCES WAS KNOWN as "the G.I.'s Nightingale," "the Armed Forces Sweetheart," and "The Sweetheart of the Fighting Fronts" for her devoted work.

"I enjoyed every minute of it," Frances said. "I could never get enough of it. And soldiers would give me messages to take back home. It was wonderful to call on the phone and tell them I just saw your husband or boyfriend. Sometimes, if they lived near Hollywood, I would go to their homes and deliver the letters in person. It was only a few days after I saw their husbands. They wouldn't believe it at first. They would read the letters and start to cry."

Sometimes she would get only three hours' sleep. Often, she washed her hair in GI helmets. "We'd flip to see who got the floor," she said, of sleeping on noisy planes with limited seats. She traveled a million miles, then stopped counting.

"They didn't have portable stages then," she recalled, "and no dressing rooms. This was the front, so who had any special accommodations for a gal?"

Jeeps of battle-weary or clean shaven soldiers would congregate and sometimes "I'd ask Bob how to read a line and he'd say, 'I'm not gonna tell you.' You had to watch him and listen and after a while you picked up the timing.

"Hope was Hope. Funny, sure, but funnier offstage than on, really. He'd send someone ahead of where we were performing to get gossip about who was in trouble with the General, then he'd drop in a joke about it for each crowd. He'd customize his jokes, and the guys just ate it up.

So many people to entertain.

"I'd sing a song, and I could just see the guys getting this faraway expression. I knew they were going home in their minds. If we were working close to the front, sometimes we'd do a show for four or five guys. It was exhausting, but it didn't matter. I was raised camping out."

Audience size never seemed to be a factor for the troupe. They did a show for seven lumberjacks in Alaska during a refueling stop once—and entertained one of their largest crowds, 100,000 GIs, in Hawaii. Though, according to an article written by Frances, she played to a *lot* more boys than that once.

Around the Camps with Bob Hope

by Frances Langford

Today the old adage, "The Show Must Go On!" has a new and very vital meaning for me. One camp tour after another with Bob Hope has convinced me how true that saying is. Time and

Singing her heart out at Hollandia on August 21, 1944.

time again the magic words, "The Show Must Go On!" have flashed into my mind, when the very last thing one might think about at the time was a laugh, a song, a few bars of music. There were too many other things to think about!

In the many months I have been away from Hollywood, one *month* for every *hour* I've appeared before the cameras, I have made a great many discoveries. I have found that no one can give too much of his or her time to entertaining the troops. Whether it is among the sanded wastes of Bizert, or in the incalculable heat and filth of a South Pacific outpost, or among the rubble-lined streets leading to Rome, the picture is the same: a heart-tugging, tear-bringing, ever-hungry reminder of the boys' insatiable appetite for anything and everything that smells of home.

That is why I have been so happy appearing with Bob Hope in all the near and far off places where these boys are, contributing my small share in the all-out effort of proving there will always be an American scene. Bright and clear in the faces of the 6,000,000 doughboys I have had the honor to sing before, the same expression has always appeared, and it reads, from the bottom of their hearts, torn with war and loneliness, **thanks**!

All and all, it is a very gratifying and satisfying thing, this business of appearing before the men of the armed forces, here and abroad. Whatever disadvantages there may be, they fade easily in the face of the happiness it brings to the boys, in the revelation of the great courage that is evidenced on every hand, and in the hard work, good sportsmanship and indefatigable enthusiasm of entertainers like Bob Hope.

In all the time I have been with Bob I have never heard him complain once. We have travelled so many thousands of miles together, and spent so many months together, that I have often been good-naturedly kidded about my long absences from home and from my own husband, Jon Hall. Even our very good friend, George Jean Nathan, went so far as to say, "Why don't you write a book of your experiences. You could call it 'My Life With Bob Hope.'

Things like that are always happening to me, but there are other things, too, that I would like to write about. Trips like these are not always the gay, amusing and glamorous journeys into foreign countries that they are put out to be. There is the other side, when terror, and strife and hardships might play so important a part. But never do, thanks to a laugh at the right moment, a gag sprung in an awkward situation, or the flair for treating a deadly serious situation lightly. Bob has that flair, as you will see.

Once, when I was singing for a wounded kid in a field hospital in Bizerte, the soldier suddenly burst out crying. I shall never forget that dreadful moment. It was at the end of the song that it happened, and I didn't know what to do. It was Bob who came to the rescue. He broke the agonized silence that followed the boy's outburst by walking up and down the beds, saying: "Fellas, the folks back home are having a terrible time about eggs. They can't get any powdered eggs at all. They've got to use the old-fashioned kind you break open."

On that occasion he had saved beautifully what might have turned out to be a very awkward situation. I shall be ever grateful for Bob Hope for things like that. He is never at a loss, come what may. And that is one of the reasons why he has so endeared himself to the American soldier, from the buck private to the highest ranking officer.

Most of all I enjoy the spirit of friendship and fun that exists among the troupe on our jaunts across the ocean. Bob, for instance, has never made any one of us feel that he is the whole works, and should be respected accordingly. Most comedians are very chary of throwing a gag the way of another member of their troupe, or even sharing a situation that might turn out to be comical. But not Bob.

Once we were at a gun emplacement center outside Tunis, and were having the time of our life looking over a big 90 field gun. The boys thought it would be fun if Bob and I fired it. I said it was all right with me, but Bob said no thanks. So I went ahead and did it myself. The concussion lifted me clear off of my feet, and from then on I acted as if I had been sampling all the wine in Italy. The boys thought it was very funny. I was a comedian for a day. And no one enjoyed the incident more than did Bob Hope, official comedian of the troupe.

The one incident I shall never forget took place in a hospital at Kairouan. In one of the beds at the dim end of the small ward, and in the shadow of a shaded window, a soldier lay very still, with a sheet up to his neck.

"This fellow is a flier," said Bob, "why don't you sing 'Night and Day' for him?"

Only "Night and Day" is a song I hate to sing in a small room, because you have to sing it so loudly. I told Bob as much.

"All right, then. Sing 'Black Magic.'"

I shook my head. "But Bob," I said, "you know it's the same type of song."

"All right, sing what you want." Bob gave me a funny look. And without saying another word, walked out. I couldn't imagine what he was driving at. Obviously, he was trying to tip me off to something but I didn't get it. So I went ahead and did my stint.

I sang, "Embraceable You!" I had arrived halfway through the song, when the soldier's lips and chin quivered. I thought, "What's wrong here?" But I didn't, couldn't guess. It wasn't long before I found out, though.

Bob was waiting for me outside. "What did you sing?"

"Embraceable you!" I told him.

He let out a groan. "I was afraid of that. I tried to tip you off, Frances, to sing something else."

"But, why, Bob?"

Bob frowned. "Well, remember in 'Embraceable You' the lines go, 'I love all the many charms about you; above all I want my arms around you?' Well, you can imagine how that guy must have felt. A couple of days ago they amputated both his arms."

One of my most thrilling experiences, however, was when I first met General Eisenhower. Almost his first words were, "I hear you've been through quite a few bombings." I admitted that we'd been through so many that we hadn't been able to sleep for several nights.

"Well," said the General, reassuringly, "you'll get a good night's sleep tonight. We haven't had a raid in three months. The Germans have had good cause to find out about our very excellent aircraft defenses, and I don't think they'll take the risk of raiding us again. You haven't a thing to worry about."

That night we gave our usual show, and after it was over we crawled into our tents, quite convinced by the good General's words that we would have an uninterrupted night's sleep. About an hour after we went to bed the siren went off. Nazi planes were black over the moonlit sky. The raid lasted for two hours and twenty minutes—the longest raid they ever had in Algiers.

At last, when it was all over, there was a gentle noise outside my tent. I asked who it was. "It's Bob," said the voice. "Are you all right?"

"I'm fine," I said. "What do you want?"

"Sh!" said Bob. "I've just seen General Eisenhower's face. It's as red as a beetroot. I thought you'd like to know. Good night."

With danger close at hand, Bob would always go out of his way to make us see the lightest side of war. And believe me, how that helped. For instance, we were checking out of Biserte in the midst of warnings of an approaching heavy Nazi raid, when Bob started to laugh. We asked him why he laughed, but he didn't tell us right away.

We had just finished stopping at the best hotel in Bizerte. In fact, it had no competition. It happened to be the only hotel still standing after the Allied shelling. Two Nazi prisoners had carried my bags into the lobby and performed sundry other hotel services for me. And that, I found out, was the reason Bob was laughing.

Finally, he said, "I was just thinking what Hitler would have said if he had seen those two Nazi supermen serving as bellhops for you, Frances!"

By that time we had left the danger zone, and once again Bob had gone out of his way to take our minds off current events. After a while we became quite used to his friendly solicitation, but knew also that when he goes to extremes to be funny without an audience we had better hold on to our hats.

It was thanks to Bob, too, that I finally got over my shyness for taking cover during air raids. I didn't want to be a sissy, and always felt that if I made a dash for the safest spot I would start getting an unenviable reputation. Thus, when we were leaving one of the desert towns in advance of an air raid, a friendly Yank bundled us in his car to get away from the populated area and where the heaviest bombing was expected.

But somehow our good Samaritan became befuddled in the darkness, and drove us right toward an anti-aircraft battery.

Enemy fighters were so close we had to abandon our car and dive for a slit trench. I felt like a sap because I was the first one out. But when I hit the bottom of the trench my fall was cushioned. You guessed it. Bob Hope had beat me to it. He was our only casualty. I fell on his thigh and gave him a charley horse.

I have yet to find out whether Bob has completely forgiven me. Perhaps I will get to know in the course of our current trip, our first to the South Pacific, Burma, India, China, and all points where the American flag marks the way to victory and that final Peace that we all want so much. I'll be seeing you!

Being the first woman to go to Alaska to entertain the boys, and the first woman to ever go to Umnack and ports on the Aleution Islands, I feel that the story of my trip from a woman's point of view may interest a lot of people.

We were only allowed to carry one bag. I was advised to take nothing but slacks and warm sweaters. I took one black wool suit and I'm very glad I did as there were a few places where I had a chance to wear it. Most of the places we visited had no accommodations for girls at all, but I soon learned not to mind that.

I was excited about going to Alaska and the Aleutian Islands, but that excitement can't compare with the great desire I have to go back again. Maybe when you read my little story you will understand why it's so very important to me.

We left Los Angeles Wednesday, Sept. 9, 1942—(Bob Hope, Jerry Colonna and Tony Romano). Tony was our guitar player. In Alaska they have very few pianos, so we took Tony along as our accompanist. All our families and friends saw us off at the airport. They seemed to think Alaska was on the other side of the world and we might never come back. I know now, those thoughts weren't so far from wrong. Had some trouble with the landing gear on the plane so we had to wait over in San Francisco for a couple of hours while they fixed it. While we were waiting, we went next door to a small army camp and gave a show for the boys. Then we were off again for Seattle, Washington. Arrived there late that night and had to wait in Seattle for two days as the weather in Alaska was bad and our plane was grounded in Juneau.

On Saturday, September 12, we took off on a Pan American plane for Alaska. Although the planes are very large, we were the only passengers aboard, due to the amount of fuel they have to carry and the extra amount of mail being carried into Alaska these days. The weather was beautiful and very smooth.

At 10:15 a.m. we left the U.S.A. and went into Canada. At 12:00 o'clock we came down at Prince George, British Columbia to gas up. We were off again in 15 minutes. Flew at 13,500 ft. for quite a while with temperature at 15 degrees below zero outside. It was necessary to use oxygen at this height. At 4:30 we stopped at Juneau, Alaska to gas up again. I think the country surrounding Juneau is the most beautiful I have ever seen. There are large glaciers running down into the rivers and breaking off, forming huge icebergs the color of the sky. Some of these glaciers flow from 4 to 5 ft. a day. The mountains are covered with silver-tipped Christmas trees, lovely lakes and waterfalls everywhere. The mountain tops are covered with snow. Here at Juneau we put our watches back one hour—off again in just a few minutes. At 4:30 we stopped at White Horse, Yukon Territory, Canada. We set our watches back another hour here. The scenery is still unbelievably beautiful. From here we went back into Alaska. Arrived at Fairbanks 6:45 p.m., 1,750 miles from Seattle. We were met at the plane by Lt. Winston Allard. Lt. Allard stayed with us for several days on our trip and was the cause of some of our happier moments. He took us to the post where we stayed while in Fairbanks. I stayed in the nurse's quarters and the boys stayed in the officer's quarters. The nurses and officers couldn't have made things nicer for us. One of the officers had been hunting and killed a large Caribou. We had roast Caribou for dinner, and it was really delicious. It tastes a lot like roast beef. The boys in the camps up here have quite a lot of Caribou and Reindeer to eat. It comes in pretty handy, especially when where is a shortage of meat.

Sunday, September 13

We gave our first show in one of the large hangers. They pushed the planes back and drove a big truck in and we gave our show on the back of the truck. The boys really did enjoy it. The morale here seemed very good and the boys all seemed quite happy. We signed several hundred autographs and stood for half an hour so the boys could take pictures. The boys were very sweet to me. They gave me a bracelet they had carved from a piece of walrus ivory that was about a thousand years old—a wonderful piece of work. After that we went into town and gave a show at the U.S.O club. The town of Fairbanks reminds me of movies I've seen of the gold rush days. It's very quaint. The prices of things are also like the gold rush days. A hamburger will cost 50 cents and a ham sandwich will cost 85 cents. After the U.S.O. , we gave a broadcast over their local station. Then back to the post for dinner. After dinner they took us out to the kennels to see the beautiful Alaskan Husky sled dogs. There were about 150 of them. These are bred with wolves and can't bark like a dog but howl like a wolf. They feed them dried salmon. In the winter time their only means of transportation are the sled dogs and the airplanes. After this we went to the hospital and gave shows for the boys in the wards. Then over to the barracks and gave another show. During the night they had an air raid alert and it was really exciting to see how quickly and efficiently things are done in an army post in an emergency. Nothing happened so it didn't last very long. That night the officers gave a dance in our honor. It was quite a surprise to see all the ladies dressed in evening gowns. I danced with a Russian Colonial but couldn't talk to him as he didn't speak English. They have quite a lot of Russians stationed here. They inspect all the planes before they are flown to Russia. The Colonel gave me 5 rubles and autographed it for me. I think I danced with a hundred fliers that night. We also gave a show here. The soldiers had quite a good swing orchestra. I went to bed about 3:00 o'clock *very tired.*

Monday, September 14

Up at 7:00 o'clock. Thought we might get an early start but had to wait for the weather to clear. From here we were given an army plane to carry us on the rest of our trip. We had a wonderful pilot, Capt. Marvin Setzer, and co-pilot, Lt. Bob Gates. Took off at 10:30 a.m. At 12:30 we stopped at Galeno. This camp is built right out in the wilds on the edge of the Yukon River. There is a village which consists of a small commissary built of logs and about four Eskimo huts. There is no diversion for the soldiers here at all. They drove a truck out to the plane and we gave a show from the back of the truck. They didn't know we were coming so they didn't have a chance to notify very many of the boys so they could bring them in from the various places where they were working. Wish we could have stayed long enough to entertain them all. While I was singing, the first snow of the year began to fall. It was quite a thrill singing in the falling snow. These boys were so happy. They said, "At last we have something good to write home about and they can't censor this." From here on we wore fur Parkas, as it was getting pretty cold. Parkas are long fur jackets with fur hoods. The hoods are made of Wolverine as it is the only fur that won't freeze when moisture touches it. We also wore rubber boots that were lined with sheepskin. They are called Mukluks. We looked like a bunch of Eskimos. Saw some more beautiful sled dogs here. Took off again about 2:00 o'clock. Arrived in Nome at 4:00. We were going to give our shows and "mush on down" to Anchorage, but a terrific storm came up on the Bering Sea, and we had to spend the night. All the boys were very happy about this, including General Jones. He is a grand person from Alabama. I can't say much for the morale here. These boys have been stationed here for two years with nothing for entertainment but a movie now and then that is always at least two years old. The food isn't the best in the world, but I guess that's because it's so hard to get supplies in here. It takes weeks and weeks for the boats to come all the way around the Aleutians up to Nome.

Nome is really an isolated place. Lots of rain and mud and cold. They have been living in tents, but the General said they are gradually getting huts built for the boys. I was in a few of those huts and they are quite warm and comfortable. The country around Nome is barren—there isn't a tree for 250 miles.

Had my first Reindeer steak at the Polar bar. It was delicious. There are lots of gold mines in operation here. I bought a lot of beautiful ivory.

Tuesday—September 15

Up at 7:00—weather cleared up nicely. Took off at 9:00. Had a beautiful trip out over the Bering Sea. Two combat planes, an AP40 and a P39 escorted us out for about 50 miles. One was piloted by Capt. Maupin, Commanding Officer of the Air Force in Nome, and the other was piloted by Carl Wade of the Royal Canadian Air Force. They did things with those planes that I didn't know was possible. They call them Pea Shooters.

Stopped over at Bethol and gave one show in the mess hall and another outside on the back of a truck on the banks of the Yukon. It was terribly cold there. From there to Anchorage. Arrived there about 5:30. As far as the post and the town is concerned, I think this is the nicest place we visited. We had a lot of fun there. We gave our first show at 6:30 p.m. and the second at 9:00. After the show I met Gen. Buckner. He invited us all over to his quarters. He is a wonderful man with a grand personality. He is the one that gave us permission to keep our same two pilots and the same plane for all our trip. Our pilots are stationed in Anchorage and their job is to fly supplies out to the Aleutians several times a week. Our pilot received a medal for bravery during the attack on Dutch Harbor.

Wednesday—September 16

We were supposed to go to Dutch Harbor but the weather in the Aleutians got very bad and flying out west was impossible. We didn't want to waste the day so we flew down to Yakutat and gave a couple of shows. From there we flew up to Cordova to give some shows. The air field is about 13 miles out of town and they have a railroad built into the town. They say it's the shortest railroad in the world. We had to ride in an open cart pulled by an engine that went at least 50 miles an hour. That was the coldest and roughest ride I have ever had.

At 9:30 p.m. we took off for Anchorage. Weather report said Anchorage was clear, but we were out about 15 minutes when we hit a terrific storm. Our pilot, Capt. Stezer, radioed back to Cordova for another report on the weather there as he thought we had better go back and spend the night there, but in those few minutes while we were gone, the weather had closed in on Cordova and it was impossible to turn back. Our only chance was to try and make Anchorage. The storm kept getting worse and worse as we were flying through sleet, and ice was getting pretty thick on the wings. One of our radios went out and it took them quite a while to get back on the beam. We finally got through to Anchorage, but we were flying at 14,000 ft.

and couldn't get down through the storm to the field. We tried several times to get down through it, but it seemed the plane would tear apart. The storm was so thick you couldn't see the tip of the wing, even when the lights were turned on. Ice was forming on the windows and it was terribly cold. Finally Capt. Setzer ordered us to put on parachutes and life belts. This thrilled me more than anything for I've always had a desire to make a parachute jump and it really looked like the time had come. Bob and Jerry [Colonna] were really surprised when they saw how excited I was. They thought I would be scared to death and probably pass out completely. We sat for one and a half hours waiting for the Captain to tell us to jump. We were running pretty low on gas by this time so Capt. Setzer radioed down to the tower at the field and told them we were preparing to abandon the ship. The whole port was out at the field by this time with all the crash wagons and ambulances ready for whatever might happen. Capt. Setzer, our pilot, hadn't looked back at us in the rear of the plane since we hit the storm. He told me later he was afraid of what he might see. He finally looked back and I smiled and he saw I wasn't afraid. He said when he saw me smile he knew he had to get us down safely—that people like us that would fly so many thousands of miles and risk our lives so many times just to make all those soldiers a little happier, he just couldn't have anything happen to them. He decided to try it once more. We literally dove straight down through the storm. I didn't know a plane could take such a beating as that one did. I thought it would tear apart. When we got a few hundred feet off the ground we saw what looked to us like a huge Christmas tree strung with lights. They had all the anti-aircraft gun searchlights pointing straight up. I know there must have been hundreds of them. Every other light on the post was also turned on to help us find the field. We landed safely and six happier people you will never see. We had quite a celebration that night and our one toast of the evening was "Thank God for our pilot—he is really a genius."

For all those people who are always asking if Bob Hope is always funny and always wise-cracking or if he reads that all off a script, I would like to say one thing—that hour and a half we were sitting there waiting to jump, not knowing if the next minute we might be face to face with death, I heard Bob make some of the funniest remarks I have ever heard in my life. He and Jerry both were very funny. It takes a lot of courage to laugh and be funny when one is in a spot like that. Our pilot said he had been in a lot of tough spots, but this was the toughest of them all and he hoped never to see another one like it. I hope he never does. I must say that experience was the greatest thrill of my life and I wouldn't take anything in the world for it.

Thursday, Sept. 19—Anchorage

Couldn't get off because the weather was still bad. We went out into the woods to entertain the boys in the dugouts. They were unable to come into the post to see our shows so we decided to go to them. They live in these dugouts. They are spread out for miles around the post, and operate the searchlights, anti-aircraft guns, and radio direction finders. The boys would come to one place from several of the dugouts, and we would give our show from the back of a truck. It was very cold and rainy. We gave five different shows out there and then we went back to the post and gave two more shows in the auditorium. There are several thousand men stationed here. Went to General Buckner's quarters again after the last show and met General DeWitt. Had a very nice party. Went back to my quarters very late, was very tired and ready for bed. My little G.I. cot looked so enticing I could hardly wait to get into it. I tried for five minutes to get into that bed, but it was impossible. I finally found out I had been short sheeted. Some of the boys had played that trick on me and I really got a big kick out of it. I had to remake the whole bed before I could get in. I found out it's an old army trick. Bob got a big kick out of it because I was the only one they pulled it on.

Friday, September 18

Left Anchorage at 10:30 expecting to go to Juneau on our way back to Seattle for our first broadcast. Stopped to gas up at a camp out in the forest called Northway. I rode in the cockpit in the co-pilots' seats most all the time. In fact, I flew the plane quite a bit. We would taxi down the runway and I would stick my head out of the window and yell, "Switches off," when we would stop. Well, when the boys standing around on the runway would see me and hear me yell, they would stand there with their mouths open and stare as if they were seeing a ghost. There are Northway they hadn't seen a girl in over a year. While they were gassing the plane, we gave a show standing on a tree stump in the edge of the forest. That was just about as cold as I've ever been. We had to stop every few minutes and rub Tony's hands to get them warm so he could play the guitar. Weather got terribly bad and instead of going to Juneau, we had to go way back up to Fairbanks.

Fairsbanks—September 19

Left early and stopped off at White Horse for gas then on down to Watson Lake. Gave two shows—one for the army boys and one for the fellows that are building the Richardson highway through Alaska. This camp is really a long ways from nowhere. There were days when these boys had nothing to eat but soda crackers. These fellows really needed a little cheering up and we certainly did our best. That night when I went to bed I could hear the wolves howling just outside. When I say wolves, I mean *animals*. Bob heard a wolf howl and he said to me, "Do you think I ought to answer back?" The wolves come into the garbage dump and they also sleep on the runway because it's warm.

Sunday, September 20

Took off at 6:45 a.m. Had to make an instrument take-off as the runway was completely fogged in. You could hardly see your hand before you. Our pilot knew we had to get back to Seattle so he said he would take off regardless of the fog. He walked the complete length of the runway so he would know exactly what he was doing and to be sure there was nothing sleeping on it that we might hit. We taxied down the runway and made one of the nicest take-offs I have ever seen. Again we said, "Thanks, Capt. Setzer, you've really become a part of our lives we shall never forget." Arrived at Seattle about 4:30 p.m. Can't say we were very happy about coming back as we hadn't done half of what we had started out to do, and we hadn't received permission from Gen. Buckner as to whether we could keep the pilots and plane and go back out to the Aleutians.

Monday—September 21

Everything seemed a little dull, waiting to hear from Gen. Buckner—no word as yet. Went out to McCord Field for the preview of our radio show. Also gave a show for the boys in the hospital. They took us to the field in station wagons through a lot of heavy traffic. I must say we prefer bad weather in our plane to this, especially when we have to be driven by a woman driver.

Tuesday—September 22

Went to Fort Lewis for our program. Although it wasn't very far we didn't like the idea of riding in those station wagons again so we decided to take our plane and fly over. I think it was about a five-minute trip, but we didn't care. It seemed good to get back in the air again. We took all the cast and writers from our show over with us. I think there were about 22 of us. Of course Bob and I had our usual fight to see who was going to sit in the co-pilot's seat, and I won out, as usual. We gave two shows and a broadcast—also one for the hospital. Got word from Gen. Buckner just before the broadcast that we could go back to the Aleutians and keep our same pilots and the same plane. He said he couldn't do enough for us as we were giving everything we had for those soldiers up there. We were so happy I don't know how we ever got through the broadcast. Flew back to Seattle and had quite a party to celebrate our trip back to Alaska and also the beginning of another season on the air. That night our two pilots, Capt. Setzer and Lt. Gates presented me with a beautiful crash bracelet. It really made me have a lump in my throat to think those boys would go out of their way to do that for me. This bracelet is just like the one all pilots have to wear.

Wednesday—September 23

Weather cleared about 12:00 and we took off again for Alaska. Arrived in Juneau at 6:00 p.m. It was good to be back in this beautiful little town again. The people up there seem to live such a happy-go-lucky life. They say once you go to Alaska, you will always go back, and I certainly believe it. When the people up there speak of going to the U.S.A., they say they are going "outside." Most of the soldiers have been in Alaska so long they call the U.S.A. the "old country."

We did a couple of shows at the camp. Stayed at the Baranof Hotel, which, by the way, is a wonderful place to stay. I think it has the only two elevators in Alaska.

Thursday—September 24

Weather cleared for take-off at 1:30. On the way out to the airport we stopped and watched the salmon going upstream to spawn. I learned that four years after a salmon is hatched it tries to go back to that same place to spawn. Only about five percent of the salmon ever reach their spawning place. The rest of them are killed beating themselves against the rocks trying to swim upstream.

After take-off we flew from 50 to 100 ft. off the water taking movies and seeing the beautiful scenery. Saw several whales and lots of beautiful icebergs. Arrived at Cordova at 4:00 for gas. Took off for Naknek out on the Aleutians. Out about 10 minutes and ran into zero-zero weather—had to turn back and spend the night in Cordova. Had to take that same rough train ride into town again. Gave a show in town and one at the hospital.

Friday—September 25

Weather cleared enough for take-off at 1:30. A navy plane that took off a couple of hours ahead of us came back and said it was impossible to get through the pass, but our pilot said we'd try it anyway and find out for ourselves—and believe me, we did. We flew almost right on top of the river going through the pass as there was hardly no ceiling at all. The mountains on either side of us ranged from 8 to 10 thousand feet. There were times when I thought the wings would touch the mountains on both sides—it was terribly rough. Ceiling kept getting lower and lower with heavy rains. This went on for quite some time, then all of a sudden we were through the pass and out over the ocean and the most beautiful weather you can imagine. Although this was one of the most dangerous spots we were in, we weren't frightened at all as we had complete confidence in our pilot. We made the Aleutians about 3:00 o'clock. Stopped at Naknek for gas—expect to be back here for shows tomorrow. Off again. Weather fairly good so we flew very close to the ground so we could see some of the wild life on the islands. Saw flocks of Ptarmigan, duck and beautiful wild swans, also herds of Caribou. Landed at Cold Boy at 5:30. Gave a show outside for several thousand men—had dinner then went to three different places, each one several miles apart and gave shows. They have their camps spread out over several miles of ground as there are no trees on the Aleutians to be used as camouflage. We stayed at General Jones' quarters that night. He was very nice to us. There are no women at Cold Bay. That night there was a beautiful full moon. The first they had been able to see up there in months due to fog. It came up behind a large volcano that erupts every nine minutes, and shown down over the Bering Sea. I've never seen a more beautiful sight.

Cold Baby—September 26

Got up at 6:00 a.m. as we had a full day ahead of us. Had breakfast and took off at 8:30. Two P40s escorted us out for quite a ways and we had lots of fun flying formation with them. Weather quite good when we left. Flew past Dutch Harbor as we expected to stop there on our way back. As we flew past Dutch Harbor the weather began to get bad again. Had rain and fog the rest of the way out west. Arrived at Umnack about 10 o'clock. We made good time on all our hops as our plane cruised at about 195 miles an hour and made as much as 250 quite a lot of the time. We were really in the war zone there. While we were circling to land there were about eight four-motored bombers taking off for Kiska. The boys told us they had a real field day out at Kiska yesterday. I got quite a thrill out of landing on those temporary steel runways. Although this is somewhat of an isolated place, the boys are really doing a wonderful job. They are all rugged, tough and healthy looking. They very seldom see the sun out there as it rains most of the time. They were all hoping the weather would get really bad so we couldn't leave. Colonel Green was very kind in letting me stay in his dugout while they built a platform outside for us to give our show on. We gave our show out in the rain while a couple thousand boys and their officers sat on the mud watching us. They really enjoyed every minute of it. General Buttler told me I was the first white woman ever to set foot on the island of Umnack. (Just had a letter from the Colonel saying the boys there are calling me Virginia

Dare Langford.) My hair is quite long and I let it hang down my back and I got quite a kick out of a lot of the boys asking me if they could just touch my hair. I was surprised when they told us we were 600 miles west of Honolulu. We went over to the mess hall and gave another show for a lot of boys. I saw something there I shall never forget. Bob introduced me and I got up on the table to sing. As I was singing my first song ("You Made Me Love You"), one of the boys in the first row began to cry. I could tell he was trying so hard not to cry. This almost broke my heart. Bob said he had seen it happen at lots of the other camps when I would start to sing. We asked some of the boys later about this and they said it wasn't because they were so terribly lonesome but just the thought of us and especially a girl traveling thousands of miles just to cheer them up. They said it made them feel that the people at home hadn't forgotten them and that they hoped they were working hard and doing everything possible to help them end this thing soon.

Had lunch with General Buttler. What a wonderful person he is. He said he didn't want us to leave but felt he ought to warn us that there was a bad storm coming up and if we didn't leave soon we might have to stay there indefinitely. Took off about 1:00 o'clock. Had quite a time getting off the ground as we had to take off sideways to the window. I thought we would never get off. Had to pass up Dutch Harbor as the weather had already closed in on it. On the way back, we saw lots of Kodiak bears. When we would see some of the bears fishing in the streams or digging clams, we would dive down on them and chase them up the side of the mountain. Some of these Kodiak bears stand from 16 to 18 ft. on their hind legs. We wasted a lot of good time chasing those bears.

All of a sudden, the weather got worse than we had seen it yet. It was just about zero-zero and we flew instruments the rest of the way into Naknek. I don't want to make things sound any worse than what they really are, but I think the people in the U.S.A. should know what those boys are fighting against up there. Three-fourths of the pilots that are killed up there are killed because of terrible weather conditions, but those boys don't complain. They say they've got a job to do and they are going to stick it out and see that it is done right. I asked our pilot if he wouldn't like to get a furlough and go home for a while. He said it would be nice to see the folks at home, but if he stayed on the job it might help to end it just a little bit sooner. If only the people here at home had a little more of that spirit, we might be better off in this war today than what we are. God knows I would gladly give my life to help end this terrible affair and send those boys home to their families and friends where they belong.

Arrived in Naknek. Had dinner and gave two shows. The boys here made me a Sergeant Major with the stripes and papers and everything. What a thrill that gave me. I feel so close to all those boys up there in Alaska, just as if I knew them all personally. I consider them all good friends of mine now.

Naknek—Sunday—September 27

Got an early start. Had a very rough trip all the way back to Juneau. After we left the Aleutians and were out over the ocean coming back to the mainland, the weather closed in on us and we couldn't see anything. We were lost for about an hour, flying about 40 ft. off the water as that was all the ceiling we had, but we weren't worried because we knew Capt. Setzer would get us in okay. Bob, Jerry and Tony slept through most of it, but not me. I didn't want to miss one minute of anything. Arrived at Juneau rather late, got a fairly good night's sleep. We really needed it.

Juneau—Monday—September 28

Weather was bad, but we left anyway. We were afraid we were going to miss our broadcast on Tuesday. Seattle was closed in completely with fog and smoke so we had to go to Spokane.

Spokane—September 29—Tuesday

That was our broadcast day and we just had to get into Seattle, but the field was still closed and our pilot could not get a clearance to land there. He got a clearance for Portland so we took off. After we passed Mt. McKinley, we were very close to Seattle. Our pilot said if we didn't get in then, we would miss the broadcast, so we decided to try and find the field and land. We came down under the fog and smoke right over the telephone wires and finally found the field. We landed and got off the field in just a few minutes. It was against the rules to land without a clearance and we wanted to get our pilots away before they got into trouble. We made the broadcast okay.

KIM STANTON, FRANCES' LAST ASSISTANT, recalled, "The major characteristic about Ms. Frances to me was her transparency regarding the war years. Every time she talked about entertaining the troops with Bob Hope and the USO, she cried. Every single time. She would talk about looking into their faces and knowing that they would be going to battle. Sometimes, she could not even speak when we discussed it or an interview was taking place. She always said it was the most important thing she did in her life and she did a lot. She always had a soft spot for the military and our troops. She held them in the highest regard always."

Bob Hope wrote, "We'd gotten into the habit of calling Frances 'Mother Langford' because she always knew what was best and was always ready with comfort and advice."

In 2007 Bob Colonna wrote in his book about his dad, Jerry:

As I write this in July of 2005, the news comes that Frances Langford has passed away at 92. The best tribute to her memory I can find comes from a letter that Bob wrote back in 1944 to the editor of the *Springfield, Ohio American*, a monthly magazine.

Dear Sir,
Just finished reading Frances Langford's story of our trips to some of the battlefronts.

On our most recent trip we toured Africa and Sicily doing four shows a day. We played in hospital after hospital, and Frances and her 115 pounds always came up smiling, regardless of whether she was playing for the troops or singing for a lone casualty in the hospital. I was right alongside of her with my 175 pounds, ready to wilt at the drop of an egg. But "Mother," as I called her in my odder moments, was always in there making the boys happy.

I've seen Frances in air raids in Africa — hiding in culverts, diving into ditches. In fact, I've beaten her into most of them. And she faces these things in the right spirit, only because she has twice as much courage as the usual allotment.

One night on our tour of Alaska, we were 13,000 feet up over Anchorage. The sleet was so thick you could have parked in mid-air, but that wasn't helping the pilot find the airport. The plane was off the beam, too, which was very unhandy. There were Frances Langford, Jerry Colonna, Tony Romano and myself, looking out of the window into that inky darkness.

Finally the crew chief said, "Stand up, Miss Langford." He put a Mae West life belt on her, and then a parachute, and said, "If you land in water, pull these two knobs."

My heart sank at that moment, because I had begged Frances to make the trip, but she looked at me with the spirit of adventure in her eyes and shrugged her shoulders as if to say, "Well, stand by; we may get a little action here." After the pilot put parachutes and life belts on all of us Frances came over and sat down and said, "If we land safely, Bob, I'll tell you something."

Well, as you know, we landed safely, or somebody else would be writing this. So I said to Frances, "What were you going to tell me?"

She said, "I was hoping we'd have to jump!"

The weaker sex!

– Bob Hope

Bob and the boys.

Frances, Bob, Jerry and the gang scouting a site to perform.

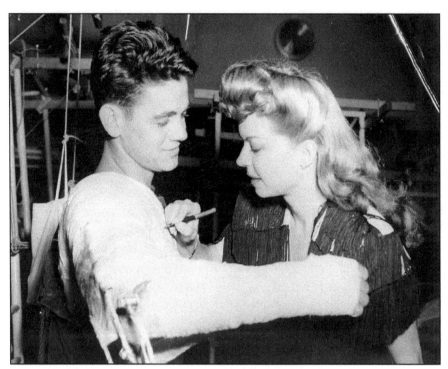

"Frances Langford takes time out to give out with an autograph at an Army hospital on Oahu. Recipient is Pvt. Charles Bessler, of Peoria, Ill., who was wounded on Saipan."

"Bob Hope and cast" says the cake. July 26, 1944.

The publicity caption reads, "FRANCES LANGFORD, golden tressed songstress has just learned from Rome, Italy that members of the American Fifth Army, many of whom she entertained in Sicily, have named her "America's Long Bob Queen." The award was made in recognition of what Miss Langford's long locks have done in the morale department for those men. Her hair-do has many times brought them mental pictures of their wives and sweethearts just when such a hypo was most needed."

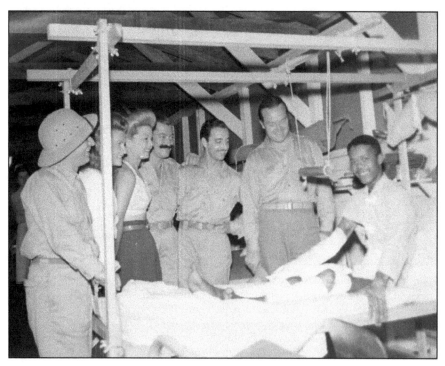

The cast visits a hospital.

The Bob Hope troupe can dish it out, and they can take it.

Singin' in the rain.

Signing for the boys.

Dibble General Hospital

Menlo Park   California

Presents this

HONOR CERTIFICATE

to

FRANCES LANGFORD

for distinguished service in the entertainment
of wounded veterans of World War II

COMMANDING OFFICER

Dated: *Nov. 1, 1945*

SPECIAL SERVICES OFFICER

With Col. Keith.

Entertaining the boys of 97 Bomber group near Tunis, Sept, 21, 1943.

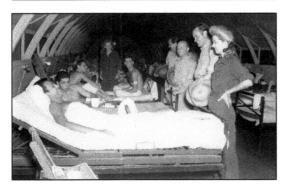

4 *Hollywood Stop*

SOMEHOW, FRANCES LANGFORD managed to make a few films in between a conservative 250,000 miles of traveling.

Mississippi Gambler (1942) for Universal was 60 minutes of gangsters, taxis and Frances singing a few songs. Wrap that all around the plot of newspaper reporter Johnny Forbes (Kent Taylor) figuring out a series of murders, starting with at a jockey at the racetrack, and you've got an hour that goes quickly. Claire Dodd, Shemp Howard and John Litel also starred. The film bears no relation to the 1953 movie of the same name starring Tyrone Power.

But the biggest picture of her career, possibly, came when she was loaned to Warner Bros. for *Yankee Doodle Dandy* (1942). The timing was right, as it was the ultimate, positive, patriotic film to showcase James Cagney (who won his Oscar for it) as George M. Cohan, the energetic showman who wrote and performed some of the best war songs ever thought up. Frances played Nora Bayes who sang "Over There" at a bond rally. Cohan, who died only months before the film's release, had many problems with the script and story, but Warner Bros. raced to complete the film in time for the ailing star. He and his wife Agnes were given a special screening just before he died. The movie's patriotic theme was a raging success for WWII audiences, even helping to sell $5 million worth of war bonds at its NYC premiere.

Cowboy in Manhattan (1943) was another quick 60-minute musical-within-a-musical for Universal starring Robert Paige, Frances Langford and several cowboy songs by Milton Rosen and Everett Carter. The packed plot involves a plethora of trouble for Broadway producer Ace Robbins (Paige) as he tries to find the money and publicity to mount his $100,000 *The Sweetheart of Texas* and keep his star, singer Barbara Lee (Langford) happy at the same time.

Irving Berlin's *This Is the Army* (1943), again for Warner, starred George Murphy, Joan Leslie, George Tobias and others. Frances sang one of three new songs that Berlin wrote for his filmed stage musical—"What Does He Look Like?"—which she performed in a café scene. She did not have a role in the plot itself. Irving Berlin himself sang one of the most famous songs, "Oh, How I Hate to Get Up in the Morning." The film was distributed for the benefit of the United States Army Emergency Relief Fund and raised almost $5 million for it through its screenings. Tickets to the New York premiere were a whopping $55 apiece. Later, the negative of the film was also turned over to the Army, on behalf of the Fund.

Back at Universal Frances would *Follow the Band* (1943) by singing "My Melancholy Baby." Based on the short story by Richard English printed in *Collier's* magazine, Frances was heard singing with the King Sisters, the King's Men, Alvino Rey and others on the Ginny Simms Radio Program. The musical comedy had a lot of music, and follows farm hand Marvin Howe (Eddie Quillan) from the Clover Leaf Dairy Farm to the top of the musical radio circuit. Frances may have received top-billing in this one, but her role was little more than a swank cameo.

The Ritz Brothers proved that there was *Never a Dull Moment* (1943) with them around. Frances was somehow able to sing "My Blue Heaven" and "Sleepy Time Gal" between their manic scenes of impersonating phony Chicago gangsters. It was unfortunately the final film in which all three Ritz Brothers appeared together.

Producers Releasing Corporation (PRC) is generally considered the bottom of the barrel when it comes to budgets and quality, but they did latch on to a lot of quality talent. Frances dived into the Stage Door-like plot of *Career Girl* (1944) to sing four numbers in this "drama, with songs." Frances plays down-on-her-luck singer Joan Terry who takes lodgings at Barton Hall where she and other talented girls ultimately put on a show in a second-rate theater and win the hearts of boyfriends and audiences alike. Edward Norris, Iris Adrian and Craig Woods also starred. The film's working title during production was *Manhattan Rhythm*.

That same year she traveled to RKO to support the comedy team of Wally Brown and Alan Carney in *Girl Rush*, a Western about the glory days of gold mining in San Francisco. Frances plays Flo Daniels, head show girl singing half a dozen songs. A young Robert Mitchum was her romantic lead.

PRC had her again for *Dixie Jamboree* (1944), a musical comedy in which Frances plays Susan Jackson, niece of Captain Jackson, skipper of the Mississippi showboat, *Ella Bella*. Amidst gangster hijinks and love with trumpeter Jeff Calhoun (played by Eddie Quillan) Frances is given several interesting songs to sing from Michael Breen and Sam Neuman. The film also starred Guy Kibbee, Lyle Talbot and Charles Butterworth. The alternate/working title of the movie was *Dixie Show Boat*.

Frances "sort of" appears in the Columbia picture, *Sailor's Holiday* (1944). It's a behind-the-studio romantic comedy that lists a lot of doubles in its extended credits. A fake Bob Hope, Loretta Young, Jimmy Cagney and many others were used. Frances' double was Linda Landi.

Then it was back to RKO for another Brown/Carney musical comedy, *Radio Stars on Parade* (1945). The studio loved the film, and promised more features starring this comedy team, but they never materialized. Frances sang "Don't Believe Everything You Dream" and "Couldn't Sleep a Wink Last Night" as Sally Baker, a nightclub singer on the lam from her gangster suitor, Lucky Maddox (Sheldon Leonard). The highlights of the film are easily the *Truth or Consequences* scenes in which Brown and Carney evade pies in the face and have to dress *quickly* as women.

Paramount's *People Are Funny* (1945) was a film version of the popular radio show created by John Guedel. The plot involved Guedel (actually played by Philip Reed) and his desperate need to create a new radio program in one week. It was the film debut for real *PAF* host, Art Linkletter, and included guests, such as Frances playing herself, reteaming her with her discoverer, Rudy Vallee.

IN THE JULY-AUGUST, 1945 issue of *The Rexall Magazine* (Frances was the cover story), Dora Albert reported, "Anyone who knows Frances realizes what she must have gone through in her visits to hospitals in Africa, England and the United States. Many times she had to steel herself not to weep at the sight of suffering. She knows that the wounded don't want pity, and so she gave them a smile, a cheerful lift of her chin, and a love song.

"She promised herself that she would never cry in front of a man in uniform. But one day she broke that vow to herself. It was when she was visiting a hospital in Africa, and met a man named Jimmy. His body was bandaged all over. Only the lower part of his face showed through the bandages. As Frances sang, Jimmy began smiling. It was a strange thing to see that smile on the face that seemed so close to death."

Frances told Dora, "What we on the home front do is terribly important to all our servicemen. No matter where on the war fronts I've visited, I have found the same thing is true of Americans everywhere. They worship American women. They idealize us. They also idealize their homes.

"When I was in the South Pacific, I was startled one day when I came to a replica of the Owl Drug Store that stands on the corner of Hollywood Boulevard and Vine Street in Hollywood. I could hardly believe my eyes—it looked so real.

"I asked the Seabees stationed there how and why they had built that familiar drug store.

"'Well,' one of them told me, 'we began to get homesick out here for a familiar scene. We began to talk about the swell times we had had in Los Angeles and San Francisco, before we sailed. We began to hunger for those familiar scenes and places. We talked of the Brown Derbies, the USO's, the waterfront in San Francisco. And finally we talked of how the corner drug stores in every city had been as familiar to us as our own homes. Somehow the drug store became for us a symbol of home. It had been a part of our lives, just as much as the roller skating rinks, the cakes that mother used to make, the smell of cookies baking on Friday afternoons.

"'We wanted to shut out the strangeness and horror and ugliness of the jungle—and bring a bit of home into our environment. That, Frances, is why we built the replica of an Owl Drug Store.'

"When he told me that, I realized that the drug stores were a symbol of home to the boys, just as Bob Hope and Jerry Colonna and Patty Thomas and I were. It's home that the boys overseas are thinking of all the time. It's the people at home—not themselves—they worry about.

"When the people at home help the war effort by donating to the War Chest, buying Bonds and donating their blood to the Red Cross, then the boys overseas are encouraged to believe that we're all back of them. When Bond sales slump and they read in the newspapers that we're not doing our share, then their morale goes down.

"At the beginning of the War, many people at home didn't realize this. It used to make me furious when I had to get up before an audience and urge them to buy Bonds. I felt that real Americans should need no urging. When people bought things on the Black Market, it used to make me see red. It still does, for I know how the boys overseas would feel about such practices.

"I know, too, how they would like to see us celebrate our national holidays or our great victories. Not with cannons roaring or firecrackers exploding… these boys have had enough noise to last them a lifetime. Their one dream, their one hope is that they may come home as speedily as possible.

"We can all help to make their dream come true. One simple easy way to do it is to buy, and hold, War Bonds—all the Bonds you think you can afford, and then some extra ones!"

"AFRICA AND SICILY were the roughest," Frances said, "because the Germans usually bombed three times a day. I guess the closest I ever came to being killed was in Africa. We were in a hospital which had been a stable, and when the raid began I went to the doorway to look. The sky was covered with flares. I know it sounds ridiculous, but it was beautiful. I was standing there, like an idiot, entranced, until someone pulled me in. The next day, we dug a big piece of shell out of the ground, and it was right in the exact place I had been standing.

"Another time we were traveling in a jeep in Bizerte when a German plane came over strafing the road. When we saw it coming, we all scattered and dove for cover. I thought I was fast, but Bob was already there ahead of me. As I jumped into the hole, I landed on his leg and he began yelling, 'I'm hit! I'm hit!' I had landed on a leg muscle and Bob had a terrific charley horse for a few days. He even turned down a Purple Heart for it.

"I think the only time I was scared was in Alaska. Our first tour in 1942. Our pilot told us that the weather conditions were so bad that we wouldn't be able to get in. He told us to put on parachutes and Mae Wests and get ready to jump. I turned cold. Just for a few seconds I was shaking. Then I thought, 'Now, this is silly. At a time like this, more than ever, you need your senses about you.' Bob and Jerry were scared green, but kept on cracking jokes. I looked over at Bob and said, 'What are you think about right now?' And he said, 'I'm thinking about all the bad shows I've ever done.'"

After an extensive tour of veterans' hospitals throughout the country, Frances returned to the United States where her adopted hometown of Lakeland, Florida named the walk around downtown's Lake Mirror: the Frances Langford Promenade. The official dedication was made during a gathering of State Governors for Lakeland's Governor's Weekend.

Returning to movies for a bit, she made *The Bamboo Blonde* (1946) for RKO. She sang "Dreaming Out Loud" in this song and dance soldier musical based on a *Saturday Evening Post* short story by Wayne

Whittaker called "Chicago Lulu" (also the film's working title). Frances plays nightclub singer Louise Anderson who enjoys national success by being painted on the side of a successful bomber plane. A fitting film for Frances.

This was also the year of her return to radio, on a little show with Don Ameche that would earn Frances a completely new legion of followers.

Russ Wade playing an Air Corps Eager Beaver in *Bamboo Blonde*, is here being attacked by his charming leading lady, Frances Langford. Tune in next week for the outcome of this ticklish situation.

Frances Langford and Patty Thomas inspect G. I. laundry ability on Guadalcanal.

Mississippi Gambler (1942).

Working for Armed Forces Radio.

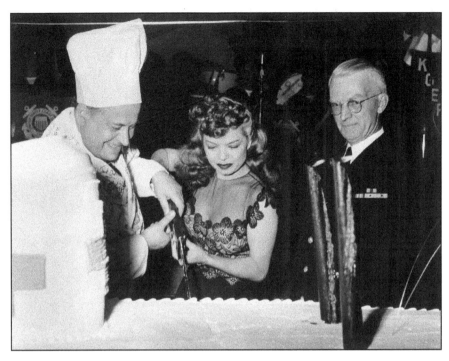

Publicity still for Rexall.

Never a Dull Moment (1943) with the Ritz Brothers.

Never a Dull Moment (1943).

Playing *The Bob Hope Show*.

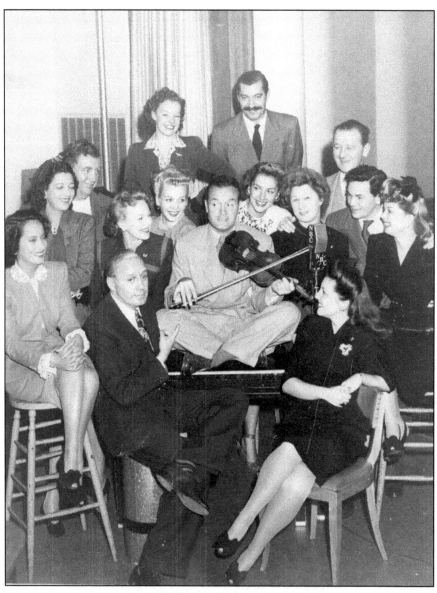

Bob Hope and the gang visit *The Jack Benny Program.*

Publicity still for *Dixie Jamboree*, 1944.

Always going somewhere.

San Diego, November 6, 1945.

At Club Brazil, Los Angeles, August 21, 1945.

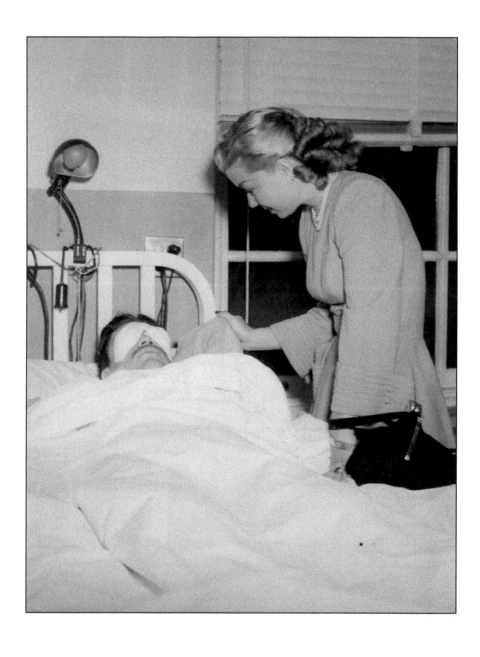

The Bamboo Blonde (1946).

The Bamboo Blonde (1946).

FL-DF-163A

5

"I'll Kiss You Goodnight In the Morning"

WHEN PHILIP RAPP'S HUMOROUS radio creation The Bickersons debuted on *Drene Time* in 1946, it was a truly original piece of business, even for its stars Don Ameche and Frances Langford who had never played this type of comedy before. No one had.

Ameche had been cast in many film roles as the hotheaded editor and the take-charge film director, so he knew how to yell with the best of them. But for singer Frances Langford, who had until then only helped with some Bob Hope gags while touring with the comic, The Bickersons was a total departure from her on- and off-screen persona.

Blanche Bickerson, quarrel-monger extraordinaire, was a complex woman and wife. She longed to be treated like a frail, loving girl, and wasn't afraid to yell like a scream queen to get it.

John Bickerson was the everyman who got nowhere. His eyes drooped, his personality clashed, and the sleepier he became, the funnier he got. He sold bowling balls, worked like a horse and slept in his shoes. But most of all… he snored like a siren or a sheepish girl, depending on his dreams.

The only time the hilarious husband and wife managed to get together for any "quality" time was at 3 o'clock in the morning when John was busy sawing wood. Blanche plead with the man to turn over on his side, which would make John scream through his nose even more, before waking up.

The characters of John and Blanche Bickerson were the sole creations of Philip Rapp, one-time writer for Eddie Cantor and Fanny Brice, and currently employed writing films for Danny Kaye. Rapp often said that he based the Bickersons on his own marital strife, sometimes gleaning a few situations (such as the bagged garbage mistaken for lunch) from activities or notions his wife Mary might initiate. Phil and Mary, who met in their early vaudeville careers, remained married for over 60 years, however, never divorcing.

No one else ever wrote a line of The Bickersons—it was all and always Philip Rapp.

Most reports put the Bickersons' origin as September 8, 1946 when the first *Drene Time* radio show aired over NBC Sunday nights at 10, sponsored by Drene Shampoo. But the first script using the Bickersons— indeed the first *Drene Time* script found in the Philip Rapp collection— was dated December 15, 1946, and obviously introduced the characters.

John and Blanche were only minutely different from what became their regular components, the most significant changes being that the Bickersons had only been married for three years; that Blanche had at one time been a schoolteacher; and that John was more deviant in his quest for some serious sleep than he would later portray: he'd bought himself a double-thick sleep shade, lullaby musical pillow, toe mittens, electric pajamas and an automatic sheep counter. (The complete script to this episode is printed in *The Bickersons Scripts* book.)

In an interview for my book on The Bickersons, Frances graciously spoke with me about her favorite role:

"One day Phil Rapp showed us the script for the first time, and asked Don, 'Do you think you could be able to snore?' And Don said, 'Sure,' and he started snoring! Just the way he did on the show!

"Phil was a wonderful director. He wrote the show, produced it and directed it. To me, he was the perfect director, perfect for what we were doing.

"My first thought when I read the first script was, *I don't think I can do this.* Because I wasn't used to that sort of thing. I was used to just a few little bits with Bob Hope which were very easy, and fun. But it gave me a chance to study timing, and I learned a lot from Bob.

"Phil was wonderful with the script and so easy to work with. The writing was the best I ever heard. For Don it was just another script, he knew he could do it. I'm sorry he had to leave us, we might still be doing it.

"Working with Don Ameche was something else. He was the greatest actor, and knew his lines: backwards. The minute he walks onto the set, he knows them. He knows his part, my part and everything. It was so wonderful working with him, and you know, he could do anything. If you can snore like that, you can do anything!

"It was awfully hard for *me* to start it. Not knowing where the laughs come, and how funny it was going to be and all, was shocking. But I wasn't shy because I was letting stuff out, getting rid of all those negative emotions. And I wasn't used to doing all that dialogue at once. Especially the medical things he talked about. They were so funny, but hard to remember. On the first broadcast, I was scared to death, and at the same time I loved doing it.

"In TV we memorized everything. And it took me a while to get used to it, but I just loved it. I practically memorized the script during rehearsals. It was easy for me like that. I only forgot my lines once, on TV. Felt like an hour, but it was only a few seconds, I guess. Live TV.

"I won as top comedian in *Who's Who* at the end of one of our years. Lucy Ball had just started but hadn't caught on yet. I don't remember getting anything like a plaque, but I wish I had something now to prove it!

"We did Perry Como's show, and three or four shows like that, because they were so crazy about it. I know Perry Como was. Jackie Gleason actually wanted to play John Bickerson. And he's funny without it. So I don't think it would've gone that well.

"When we started, Danny Thomas was playing my brother, Amos. But the Bickersons were getting all the laughs without Brother Amos. Danny was with another agency who had plans for him to be much bigger, which he was later. They took him off our show and started him on his other career. It just wasn't the part for him.

"Don was hard to replace. If he was making a picture or something, they had to get somebody else. There wasn't a lot of rehearsal for Don and I but if we had another person, there was quite a lot. Lew Parker was wonderful. But he was a different kind of John.

"Blanche is my bad side coming out, and I got rid of it that way. She's a terrible person. John was so hen pecked and brow beaten. and her voice alone would just about wear him out. It was a pretty rough marriage. John had to work an awful lot, and I was always buying the wrong things. It would've been very funny if they'd visited a marriage counsellor. I think it would've done them good. I think Phil could have made something good out of that. Blanche would've *made* him go.

"There weren't many negative letters through the years. Maybe some people didn't like the fighting, but maybe that's because *they* were doing it.

"I remember it was difficult to keep the set quiet. The crew really wanted to laugh. And that was really hard to do. We had to have quiet on the set, and it was almost impossible.

"I'd rather do the Bickersons than sing–any day. There are just as good today as when we first performed them. The people are still laughing at it. Everywhere I go. And I don't blame them. I loved doing it. People I know who have children, it's the children who say, 'Let's play The Bickersons.' Because it's the same house and home life that we had way back then, and even now."

THOUGH FRANCES WASN'T MAKING many films these days, she did return to RKO for *Beat the Band* (1947) with Gene Krupa and his band. It was based on the Broadway musical of the same name, with book by George Abbott and music by John W. Green, and lyrics by George Marion, Jr. Though, as usual with Hollywood, the original songs were tossed out and new songs tossed in. The plot was a tiny bit like Frances' own life: small town girl wants to be an opera singer, but during her lessons she turns into a big band singer. She performed her three songs with panache: "I've Got My Fingers Crossed," "I'm in Love," and "Kissin' Well" (all written by Leigh Harline and Mort Greene).

The next year she was a part of a musical variety cartoon that the Disney corporation rarely mentions anymore, except in chopped up form. *Melody Time* (1948) was part live-action and part animation. It was a wonderful collection of cartoons telling the stories of Johnny Appleseed (narrated/sung by Dennis Day), Little Toot (handled ably by the Andrews Sisters), the story of Pecos Bill (narrated by Roy Rogers and the Sons of the Pioneers), among others.

Frances sings the beautiful ballad, "Once Upon a Wintertime" (written by Bobby Worth and Ray Gilbert) over a cartoon short showing the courtship of two young lovers who take to skating in the "olden days." The film's working title was *Sing About Something*.

In 1944 Walt Disney had announced plans to make a feature-length cartoon called *Currier and Ives*, to be based on the famous print collection, and that he was planning to hire Frances as well as "the maestro of the Maxwell House Coffee program," Al Sack, to compose the musical score. But *Melody Time* was as far as *that* idea progressed.

Deputy Marshal (1949) was the only time Frances and husband Jon Hall appeared on screen together, though a stream of many pictures were announced. It was an independent picture for Lippert Films. Based on the novel of the same name by Charles Heckelmann, the plot involved Federal Deputy Marshal Ed Garry (Hall) after a couple of bad men (Joe Sawyer and Dick Foran). Garry is also trying to protect Janet Masters (Langford) from the thieves trying to steal her valuable property now that the new railroad's coming through. Frances sang the film's only two songs, "Hideout in Hidden Valley" and "Levis, Plaid Shirt and Spurs."

Columbia producer Sam Katzman had announced to the press that he had wanted Frances and Jon to star in the India adventure, *Last Train from Bombay* (1952), but only Jon made it. The female lead went to Christine Larson.

Frances did appear in the fun variety comedy, *Make Mine Laughs* (1949), a 7-reeler for RKO, which starred Ray Bolger, Joan Davis, Dennis Day, Jack Haley, Leon Errol. Frances sings "Moonlight Over the Islands" early in the vaudeville show that is essentially the whole plot. It was really a combination of other RKO films, including *George White's Scandals* and *The Bamboo Blonde* (from which Frances' song was taken), along with new material. When both Bolger and Haley sued the studio for using their names in the film without their permission, cash settlements were made and the film was forced out of distribution.

ON JANUARY 29, 1950 Frances received a citation from the 109th Anti-Aircraft Artillery Brigade of the Illinois National Guard "for outstanding services in entertaining the troops in the Pacific" during the war. "I've never felt that persons in my category merited citations," she told the press. "I've always believed such honors should go to the boys who did so much for our country. But since others feel I do deserve the citation, I am deeply grateful. I thank you."

She also made headlines that year when it was reported on May 12th that Frances met President Truman in Coulee City, Washington about the prepared closing of the Birmingham Hospital in Van Nuys, California. She'd sent the President a telegram about meeting to discuss it; she wanted five minutes of his time. But she was so surprised when Truman cut her plea short by saying, "The whole thing's a pressure cooker and I won't have a thing to do with it!" Then he took her by the arm, moved her to the side, and greeted the next person in line. Frances was so surprised, she couldn't speak. Later, she told the press, "He was so cordial to me at the White House. But I think he is burned up about the matter and doesn't want to talk about it."

Immediately after that, Frances was photographed for papers with some of the hundreds of letters and telegrams she received following her "brushoff," which overwhelmingl y cheered her position. One man from Chicago wrote, "We are with you 100 per cent. If Frances Langford, who sang in the foxholes for the boys, received such a reception from our President, I resign as a Democrat."

Frances told the press, "I don't mind that the President snubbed me. What hurt was that he was really snubbing the paralyzed veterans, the tuberculars and other boys at Birmingham. I was only going to ask Mr. Truman questions they would have asked!" As this was at the same time that Frances was penning her "Purple Heart Diary" column in a stream of William Randolph Hearst newspapers, it was certainly an unwise move by the President.

She wrote:

May 16, 1950—It's easy to spot the agony, anguish and monotony which are part of the long hedgerows of misery called hospital wards.

Less apparent are the broken dreams, but no less injurious are they to the health and morale of the hospitalized victims.

Many of those dreams were born in verminous foxholes during World War II. Ads used to carry their counterpart—the picture of a uniformed soldier and his bride fondly gazing at their dream home.

Up until a few days ago some of the owners of those damaged dreams, men paralyzed from the waist down, thought their heart's desire had paid off.

They thought they would never have to worry about housing again. Spelling security for them were their specially constructed homes in San Fernando Valley—homes easily accessible to a much-needed treatment center, Birmingham Veterans Hospital, and containing all the appointments designed to meet the therapeutic and comfort needs of these terribly handicapped fellows.

Then came the bombshell that has them still picking up the pieces of their dream. President Truman, no stranger to veterans' problems, had ordered the closing of Birmingham and the transfer of its patients and facilities to Long Beach Naval Hospital.

Thus was tossed into their laps a hopeless situation—one pregnant with bewilderment, discouragement and bitter disillusionment.

Already suffering from war's most devastating injury, they must absorb the additional shock of having to either sacrifice their homes or drive 80 miles round trip through areas heavily choked with vehicular traffic, including an endless parade of heavy trucks.

When, Mr. President, are we going to stop economizing at the expense of those who shed their blood and gave their health for our liberty?

Is losing their homes going to be their reward for sleeping in dirty, stinking foxholes while those at home had nice, clean, safe beds?

Is our big-hearted generosity to be confined to Friendship Trains and Marshall Plans? Can't the same people whose hearts are always bleeding for Europeans, including our former enemies, do a little worrying about these grievously maimed and permanently incapacitated displaced-persons-to-be?

May 18, 1950—Since receiving the presidential brushoff at Coulee City I have seen many anxiety-ridden faces at Birmingham Veterans Hospital. Such has been the sad aftermath of Mr. Truman's order to transfer them to Long Beach Naval Hospital.

For the first time since their hospitalization began they are afraid to face the future. This doesn't mean the flame of their courage has been extinguished. You can still see it burn fiercely in their eyes.

But then Jack Dempsey was a nervous, fear-stricken man before the first round gong clanged.

This fear of Birmingham's patients, especially that of the paraplegic men with homes near the hospital, is gaining momentum. It's spreading among the families and friends of these war-battered ex-heroes.

The patients' spirit is so crushed that a few of them say they'll flatly refuse to go to Long Beach for the frequent treatments they must have to stay alive.

They have told me they would rather risk an early death than either give up their homes or travel 80 miles round trip to Long Beach. The word risk is theirs. Inevitable would be my choice.

"Honestly, Miss Langford," one of them told me, "I don't care what happens to me."

This issue is no longer one of cold-blooded economics alone. We must view it in terms of human life, rather than dollars. To do otherwise would be an act of great cruelty and inhumanity.

Birmingham's removal is a deal that is assuredly not consistent with the innate decency and generosity of the American people.

For, thank God, we're still living in a country where the people make the laws. And where the people can decide what kind of a deal our sick and disabled veterans shall have.

Hollywood, May 20—Any psychologist will tell you that there is nothing worse for your mental attitude than a hopeless dilemma.

The human spirit is capable of meeting the most rugged of challenges. But it can't get to first base unless there's a way out of a situation—so long as there is hope.

For the past few days I've been talking with a group of men whose hopes have been killed by such a predicament. They are tubercular veterans at Birmingham Veterans Hospital. Like their paraplegic buddies, these men face untold hardships as the result of the abandonment of Birmingham.

While battling the awesome tuberculosis microbes, they are continually hearing about bedrest and emotional rest. Impressed on them is the fact that one without the other is of little benefit.

Living in the shadow of Birmingham's closing, however, they can't see how any kind of rest is possible for them in the future. For they, too, face the loss of the homes they built near Birmingham because of the taxing 80-mile round trip trek to the new tubercular treatment center at Long Beach Naval Hospital.

In a few days we'll be observing another Memorial Day. It's the day when we say some mighty kind words about the men who didn't come back from battle.

I wonder how these words will taste in the mouths of these Birmingham evictees who, fighting to keep the holes of death in their lungs patched up, must trade the warm and dry climate of San Fernando Valley for the coastal cold, fog and dampness of Long Beach.

I'm sure that this isn't the deal for which their fallen comrades died. The great tragedy of their heroic death is that they didn't have a real chance at life. I wonder if we aren't adding to that tragedy by denying that chance to those who came back.

Seattle, Wash., May 22—Judging from the many letters I have received, the gloom hanging over Birmingham Veterans Hospital isn't confined to Southern California.

Hospitalized war veterans in other parts of the country are starting to worry whether they too will be the victims of future closure orders.

Like the paraplegic and tubercular patients at Birmingham, many of them have established homes adjacent to a veteran's hospital. This is so they can be near their families during periods of protracted hospitalization and near a treatment center when they become out-patients.

Still in the throes of rebuilding their health, this fresh worry won't help but bring them psychological and physical setbacks.

According to their letters, the thing that is hurting them most is their utter confusion. They can't understand why Uncle Sam keeps ducking his moral and patriotic obligation to them and their buddies.

The same king-sized enigma has haunted me ever since the shooting stopped.

Billions of dollars are being squandered in an orgy of global philanthropy, but in good old U.S.A. we count our cents where our own disabled veterans are concerned.

You don't bargain with the doctor when your child falls ill. You don't count the cost of treatment. Your mind is too full of prayer that he will get well.

That's the attitude the Government should take toward the rehabilitation of our war-mauled heroes.

Neglect, inappreciation and ingratitude are ugly traits. They must not be allowed to become part of the American way.

Seattle, May 27—President Truman's eviction notice to several hundred paraplegic and tubercular patients at Birmingham Veterans Hospital still stands.

For Washington's new plan for the hospital falls far short of insuring that the paraplegics' homes near Birmingham will be saved, and it cruelly ignores the turberculars who are in the same boat.

It definitely shouldn't stop you from continuing to register your protest against the President's ill-advised closure order.

When you write the President, remember that his mind is completely closed to a review of this case. But I don't think his heart can be likewise shut.

So I'd like to suggest that you attach to your letter these lines from the pen of a Gold Star Mother, Mrs. E. D. Vang, of 4823 Riverton Avenue, North Hollywood, Calif.

"Dear Miss Langford: I know how very much Birmingham is needed in this valley.

"When my own son was brought there, the TB wards were so crowded extra beds had to be added.

"He was a good, strong boy when the Navy took him. They gave him back to me, to put in a TB ward. He's the only boy I have left out of three beautiful boys.

"No wonder we over 60 are dropping off like flies from heart trouble. The President is putting so much on these old hearts we cannot take it.

"All the mothers and fathers I know are back of you, dear girl, 100 per cent. Keep on fighting as you have in the past. If the President gives you the go by, God will not. May God give you the strength and courage to go on."

Thank you, Mrs. Vang. I'm sure God will give us all strength and courage to continue this fight until it's won. For none of us will have peace of mind until it is completely won.

Langford sings under strange difficulties in this scene from RKO Radio's musical, "Beat the Band," and Phillp Terry leads Gene Krupa (at the drums) and his band in a hotel boiler room. Miss Langford, Terry, Ralph Edwards and Krupa are starred.

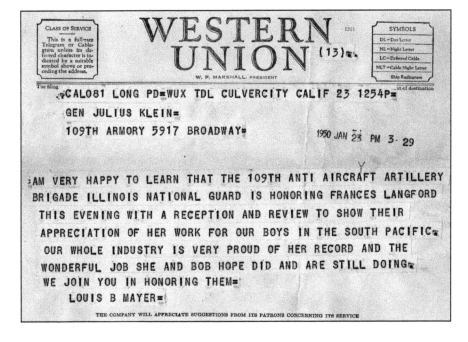

Don and Frances.

With Mrs. Helen D. Gilbert, National President of American Legion Auxiliary.

Ward #9 at the U.S. Veterans Hospital, San Fernando, AZ, March 1947.

BTB-PUb-A13

Frances and husband Jon in *Deputy Marshal* (1949).

6

Bye, Bye, Hollywood

FRANCES MADE THE PAPERS again in 1950 when was signed to a 5-year contract with Columbia Pictures Studio for ten "top-budgeted films… in a series of pictures depicting the down-to-earth experiences of a typical American girl." She was shown, smiling, signing the contract while producer Sam Katzman looked on. This promotion closely followed husband Jon Hall's own 5-year contract, when he was also signed by Katzman. The first picture was to be *Hurricane Island*, which was slated to go into production in the Fall of 1950.

On October 3, 1950 Paramount released the documentary *Cassino to Korea* which used frontline WWII footage from the Army Signal Corps to trace the course of the American campaign in Italy. Jack Benny, Bob Hope, Joe E. Brown and Frances made brief appearances entertaining the troops, though much of the film involved reenactments of Italian battles and material from captured German, Italian and Japanese combat films. War correspondent Quentin Reynolds narrated the film.

When her Katzman contract failed to materialize, Frances turned to television, as most radio actors did at the time. With Bickersons co-star Lew Parker she hosted *Star Time*, an hour-long variety series which had heaps of songs, sketches and Bickersons. It only lasted four months, ending in February of 1951.

The following is an excerpt from the 4th *Star Time* episode, broadcast on December 26, 1950.

THE BICKERSONS

> ANNOUNCER
> And now, ladies and gentlemen, here are Frances Langford
> and Lew Parker as John and Blanche Bickerson in "The
> Honeymoon is over."

THEME: (SOFT AND PLAINTIVE)

> ANNOUNCER
> Blanche Bickerson has finally realized her fondest dream,
> a new and larger home. It is past midnight and the
> moving man is carting the last of the Bickerson's belong-
> ings into the spacious six room apartment as the watchful
> Blanche supervises the unloading.

FADE IN new Bickerson apartment.

Blanche in her hat and coat, stands in the middle of the room.
All about the place are signs of having just moved in. A barrel
stands near the dresser—two suitcases are by one wall—a
carton is piled on top of the suitcases. The moving man, in
overalls is bringing another barrel into the room.

> MAN
> Where do you want this, lady?

> BLANCHE
> Leave it right there for the time being.

> MAN
> Yes, ma'am.

> BLANCHE
> I never realized we had so much stuff. Isn't it funny
> how people hang onto all kinds of junk?

> MAN
> Yes, ma'am.

BLANCHE

I guess all married people are like that. Are you married?

MAN

No, ma'am. I look this way from carryin' heavy furniture.

BLANCHE

Oh. Are there any other large pieces on the truck?

MAN

Yes, ma'am. I gotta bring the stove up. They shoulda give me another man to help me.

BLANCHE

I thought my husband was helping you. Where is he?

MAN

I ain't seen him since I took his bed apart at your old place. It wasn't easy with him still in it.

BLANCHE

Well, my husband works very hard and he needs his sleep.

MAN

I didn't wake him up. I propped him against the wall with a bedslat. He was gone when I come up for the barrels.

BLANCHE

Well, he's probably down at the truck. You go get the stove.

Man exits carrying dolly. Blanche picks up carton, starts toward kitchen and stops suddenly as she reaches the barrel. From inside the barrel comes the sound of John's snoring. Blanche stares, then pulls the sheet off.

JOHN (snores and whines)

BLANCHE

John Bickerson! What are you doing in that barrel?

JOHN (a protesting whine)

Mmmmmmm.

BLANCHE

Get out, get out, get out!

JOHN (putting his head out.
He wears a hat)

Get out, Blanche. Wassamatter? Why don't you let me sleep?
Whaddya want, Blanche?

BLANCHE

Get out of that barrel! I'll bet you've broken all my
dishes!

JOHN

Only one.
    (he hands her a chafing dish)
Here.

BLANCHE

What did you do that for? You broke the handle off my
chafing dish.

JOHN

Well, it was chafing me. Goodnight.

WHEN *THE BICKERSONS* finally got its own standalone radio show (a
full 30 minutes of Bickersons plot, nothing else), the July 7, 1951 issue of
Cue magazine wrote that "Lew Parker…is every bit as good as Ameche—in
fact, we begin to believe that almost any actor-comedian with expert time
sense and a loud, fast and belligerent delivery would be pretty satisfactory
in the role. Parker has all three of these, and he's swell.

"Miss Langford, we'd like to wager, is the indispensable one. This
role of Blanche Bickerson started a whole new phase of her career, and

brought her a new public. She's even won a couple of top comedienne polls, which is as it should be. She has a wonderful way with the nagging, complaining lines, and also that necessary time sense that has to be a part of top comedy."

Returning to film in that same year, it was perhaps fitting that one of Frances' last screen outings should be for a Columbia movie based on her own writings. *Purple Heart Diary* (1951) was a WWII melodrama, and was intended to be a bit biographical, about her wartime exploits. She plays herself during a USO tour of the Pacific with singers Ben Lessy and Tony Romano. Mostly it tells the story of how she helps her military liaison and guide, Lt. Mike McCormick (Judd Holdren) deal with his lost leg and ultimately accept his much-deserved Purple Heart. The film was shot in only 9 days, from June 4 to June 12, 1951.

From September 10, 1951 to March 14, 1952 Don Ameche once again joined Frances, this time for the daytime variety series, *The Frances Langford-Don Ameche Show*. The ABC series also featured Tony Romano and his orchestra, and a young Jack Lemmon and Cynthia Stone in a running sketch called "The Couple Next Door." It ran for 135 performances.

Then, in 1953, Frances was doing her patriotic bit again. This time in Korea. Again with Bob Hope, they were bringing joy and laughter to an otherwise joyless time in American history.

When Frances, Bob, her husband Jon Hall, comedian Wally Vernon, comedienne Ginger Sherry, dancer Margaret Brown and three musicians returned from their six-week tour of Korea on October 21, 1953, Frances told the press, "Our boys aren't concerned whether we call it a police action or anything else. The Chinese reds are firing real bullets and our men are bleeding real blood."

They covered practically every foot of the 155-mile front where they entertained over 250,000 troops, visiting every division and unit in combat areas, hospitals, camps, hospital ships, and on Koje Island which held 100,000 war prisoners.

One show was given on Hokkaido, a northern island of Japan, 14 miles from the coast of Russia. Another was so close to the enemy guns of "Old Baldy" (a vicious series of battles in west-central Korea) that the makeshift stage shook. After the show, Frances and Jon went to the bottom of the hill to talk to the gunners. She told the *L.A. Times* later, "We were really scared to learn that we were really lucky that the Reds weren't firing back just then.

"They didn't anticipate so many casualties, and blood supplies are very low. The soldiers are griping about the lousy food the way they did in World War II. Food is good now, but they have a new complaint. They think Americans at home pay more attention to sports events than the war."

Dining with Bob.

Korea, 1952.

Korea, 1952.

7 *A New Love*

FRANCES FOUND A LOT of work in the variety craze of early television. When Bob Hope hosted *The Colgate Comedy Hour* on December 7, 1952, Frances and Tony Martin joined him to sing "A Fine Romance." She also appeared the following year on the game show, *The Name's the Same*, and in December she was seen on *The Jackie Gleason Show* singing "Great Day" and "I Love Paris."

But she left her Hollywood career with a bang. *The Glenn Miller Story* (1954) was her final film, though she was only in a single scene. She appeared with The Modernaires and the Glenn Miller Orchestra entertaining the overseas troops in World War II. The film was a financial and critical success, and was nominated for several Oscars, including Best Music and Best Writing, and won for Best Sound Recording.

On April 17, 1954 Frances confirmed to the press that she and husband Jon were now separated, after 16 years of marriage. She didn't elaborate on the estrangement, but said they had no immediate plans for a divorce. Hall's attorney told the press that "their separate careers" was the reason for their breakup. And Frances admitted that the separation wasn't a new thing: "I've been on the road a long time." She was currently touring the nightclub circuit all across the country. "Our marriage lasted," she said, "because we had the same mutual interests. We both liked planes, and we owned a GI school in Santa Monica where planes could be chartered or rented."

On August 29, 1955 the press reported that Frances and Jon had obtained an amicable divorce in Titusville, Florida. Frances had filed the suit "some time ago," but the grounds had not been disclosed.

Meanwhile, Frances had met Ralph Evinrude during her nightclub tour. She was singing in Milwaukee and the 48-year-old Ralph was sitting in the audience, falling in love. "It was the last show," she said, "and the owner came up and asked me to go meet Mr. Evinrude at his table. 'You know I don't do that,' I said." But Ralph came up to her and offered to take the entire company out for bacon and eggs. "The six of us went to his home. It was very late—after the last show—but there he was in the kitchen, fixing eggs, bacon, toast. He kept getting nicer and nicer. From then on, that was it.

"I didn't want to ever marry again, but he was such a sweet man, a kind man—different from people in Hollywood. And because of my own background in Lakeland, we had things in common: boats, the outdoor life. He was crazy about music. And he liked my singing. That was important."

Ralph S. Evinrude was born in 1907, the year his father built a prototype of the first (mass market) outboard motor. He attended the University of Wisconsin while also working at the Elto Outboard Motor Company, run by his parents (Ole and Bess), and was home every weekend. He left school in 1927 to assist in the development of a new four-cylinder motor, the Elto Quad. He stayed with the family business for the next 55 years. Their slogan: "Don't row—throw your oars away."

At the age of 27, he became president of the company, after having worked in the engineering and marketing departments, when his father died in 1934. He put in 14 hour days during World War II managing the company's production of war equipment and spent his evenings and weekends working for the Coast Guard at Lake Michigan. During his time as Chairman of the Board in the 1950s, he solidified the family business as a Fortune 500 company. The company offered the public everything from lawn care products to remote controls to fully-enclosed engines. By the time he finally retired in 1982, the Outboard Marine Corp. was employing 9,000 workers throughout the world.

BUT BACK IN 1955, Frances was a little too honest with her new beau. She told him that she thought there were better outboard motors, like the Johnson motor, than the ones he made. He loved her honesty—and told her that he owned the competition's company, too.

"I fell for her just like that," Evinrude said. "It was her love of fishing and the water that brought us together. And what a fisherman. The rougher it gets, the better she likes it. She even has her own skiff for fishing."

On October 6, 1955 Frances married Ralph aboard his yacht, *The Chanticleer*, which was cruising in Long Island Sound. They stopped in Flushing Yacht Basin for media photos; the wedding photos showed the happy couple cutting the tall wedding cake together. Thirty friends were in attendance, with the Rev. Joseph Huntley of the Broadway Congregational Church of New York City performing the ceremony. Charles Z. Wick, Frances' manager, gave the bride away, and her friend and secretary, Mary Kellogg, was the Maid of Honor.

It was Ralph's third marriage—he had two children from his first marriage. Ralph fell in love with his wife's Florida just as much as Frances had, so they moved to the 400 acres around Jensen Beach that Frances had begun amassing since 1936, when she first bought a 100-acre land parcel for $15,000. "I always wanted someplace where people couldn't move in on me," Frances said. Ralph built a motor testing division on the north side of the St. Lucie River, to tinker with his engines, and adopted Martin County as his own base of operations. There they lived, with Ralph commuting to Waukegan, Illinois where Outboard Marine's headquarters was located.

Though after Ralph's retirement in Jensen Beach, the couple spent much of their time aboard their 118-foot yacht, *Chanticleer*. But still he kept his hand in things, heading up three philanthropic foundations and founding the Florida Institute of Technology's Ralph Evinrude School of Marine Technology.

The *Chanticleer* was big enough for a CinemaScope screen on which Frances showed her favorite musicals to friends. On the walls were some autographed photos from friends: Reagan, Churchill, Nixon, Eisenhower. Behind the bar, engraved on the mirror, were bars of music from "I'm in the Mood for Love," her biggest hit of WWII.

"I take plenty of exercise," she said. "I do a lot of walking, swim a lot." She also fished a lot. "I think everyone should be a fisherman. It's a quiet and wonderful, simple life. It doesn't matter—you can take a picnic lunch with you, fish all day. Sometimes the fishing is great, and sometimes not. Either way, it's fun. One time, I caught a Bluefin tuna off the Bahamas. They measured it and said it would have been 750 pounds if sharks hadn't have attacked it as I was pulling it in! The head alone weighed 414 pounds."

"Yes, she loved to fish," explained Kim Stanton. "She would schedule fishing trips throughout the year. She had a fishing boat with its own crew that would go along with the yacht to various spots in the Bahamas.

She would also take the yacht across the state of Florida through inland waterways (Okeechobee Waterway) to the west coast of Florida. Sometimes she would travel down to the Dry Tortuga's.

"She was also a member of the Cat Cay Club. Mark Perry of the Florida Oceanographic Society here in Stuart has many of the fish she caught hanging on the wall at the FOS."

In one of the last newspaper interviews she gave, Frances said the fish on the wall of the FOS showcased over 20 of her catches, including that Bluefin tuna head, and a 370-pound marlin. They were part of a "name the fish" computer game for children. She also donated her Stuart beach house to the FOS in 1989 as part of their $6.5 million expansion project. They sold the prime real estate and netted more than half a million dollars.

The Evinrudes had a 48-foot sportfishing boat that followed the *Chanticleer* on most trips. "We use the Boston Whaler," Frances said. "It's small and light, to take the dog into shore, or to the other boat," she explained. Beau was their white poodle, on board all of their cruises.

They bought a tiny island in Baie Fine in one of their favorite lakes in Canada's Georgian Bay. It was where Ralph spent his childhood summers. On "Evinrude's Island" was just a cabin, with two fully-stocked refrigerators. The *Chanticleer* would be docked there for a full month. The island was only about 50 feet across and 100 feet long. "We just plug in our boat for electricity," Frances explained.

In winters they would cruise the Caribbean and fish in the Bahamas or Dry Tortugas at the end of the Florida Keys. Ralph also taught his wife how to fly, and she became a licensed pilot.

In a brochure for Frances' restaurant, The Outrigger, there was also a lengthy article on

THE YACHT CHANTICLEER

The striking 118' yacht *Chanticleer* is the centerpiece jewel of the Outrigger Marina. Featured in *Legendary Yachts* by Bill Robinson, the *Chanticleer* was the first of six sister yachts built in 1947 by DeFoe Shipbuilding in Bay City, Michigan.

Named *Chanticleer* by the original owner, the yacht was purchased by Ralph Evinrude in 1953. With a beam of 18 ½', and drawing only 6 ½' the yacht is capable of cruising the inland waterways as well as making ocean voyages.

Four GM six-cylinder diesel engines, painted white with chrome trim, are hooked up in tandem, two for each propeller on the twin screws, and the 4,000 gallon fuel tanks offer a cruising range of 2,000 miles, at a cruising speed of 12 to 14 knots, burning 35 gallons per hour, including operation of a 30 kw. generator.

Retractable, anti-roll stabilizers cut roll from thirty to three degrees. Bow jets shoot 1,000 gallons of water per minute at 80 pounds of pressure, enabling the *Chanticleer* to move sideways when maneuvering in the water. There is also a desalinization plant to change sea water into drinking water.

On the lower deck, there are four double staterooms with toilet and shower in each, and crew quarters for eight, though the yacht generally carries a crew of six.

On the main deck, there is a formal dining room that seats 10, a comfortable lounge with a wet bar and piano, a large lounge that converts into a theatre for motion pictures, and an open after-deck at the stern. The yacht is air conditioned throughout, and five television sets operate off a rotatable antenna.

The top deck features the pilot house, containing every modern electronic device, including two radar sets, loran, depth-sounder, long range radio-telephone, every kind of safety alarm, including electric and manual steering, and gleaming engine controls, all the pride of the master yachtsman.

Behind the pilot house are two tenders, a 14' with a 75hp Evinrude outboard, and a 17' with a OMC stern drive. Nine outboard engines of differing horsepower are lined up, used for testing purposes. They are the next year's models that Evinrude tests on his summer trips to Canada.

There is a fifteen man life raft which inflates automatically, equipped with flares, radio, food and water for two weeks, fishing tackle and other emergency necessities.

The remainder of the top deck to the stern is a sitting area for sunbathing or relaxation.

Ralph Evinrude wooed and won Frances Langford on the *Chanticleer*, and they were married in the dining room in 1955 at Port Washington, New York. The yacht is their second home, and they have traveled extensively, including trips north as far as Nova Scotia, the St. Lawrence, Great Lakes, Mississippi, all ports in the Caribbean, through the Panama Canal and up to Los Angeles, and to South America.

Their most challenging voyage was in 1965, to Europe, most Mediterranean ports, the Black Sea, the north and west coasts of Africa, and return. The trip took six months, and was flawless.

When cruising the Gulf of Mexico, the Evinrudes bring along the *Fran E.*, their Norseman sportfisherman.

Mr. Evinrude has made the *Chanticleer* his dream yacht, from the red carpet for guests visiting his gleaming white and chrome engine room, to the artificial tree they bring along for their poodle.

Around 1988 they built a second *Chanticleer*, actually the former *Buckpasser*, built in 1973 for Ogden Phipps. They decided to rechristen it the *Chanticleer* since Phipps was passing his famous racehorse's name on to his own new vessel. The original *Chanticleer* was given to a college, as it was getting a little old by then, which sold it Samuel du Pont, thus returning it to the family of the original owner. "I gave them everything we had from the boat to make it look the way it did," Frances said. "They are so proud of it and it's so beautiful."

Frances fell in love with the *Buckpasser*'s interior colors of rusty red and forest green. Paola Smith gave the 98'6" vessel an extensive refit at Bradford Marine in Fort Lauderdale. It took 11 months. It was lengthened for a swimming platform and breezy open aftdeck. Portholes were elongated, and the mast was stylishly raked. What was once a helicopter deck became a lovely steering station with wicker seats. The open lounge was converted into a large teak dance floor. It also left room for extra tankage: 5,000 gallons of fuel, and two reverse osmosis water makers that could produce 1,000 gallons of fresh water daily.

Paola used Frances' trademark "I'm in the Mood for Love" as a "musical accent" to the new yacht's décor: musical notes punctuated by hearts in the bar mirror, on the napkins, pennant, and shirts worn by the crew. There were quarters enough for a crew of six, which was their usual crew number when traveling North. There were four staterooms for guests, and the latest in electronics for safety ("You can never have enough safety equipment," Frances said). Also, a big-screen Pro-Scan TV with satellite antenna so no matter where they were, it would scan and keep the signal solid. It also provided location coordinates so that CDs, radio or TV could be piped to any location on board.

Frances had a way with boats. Her boat captain Karan Haddad explained, "You know, she would call me on the house phone, even in the middle of the night, and let me know if the engines were out." Though the cruising speed of the vessel was between 12 and 15 knots, their usual jaunt to Canada kept them at about 10 knots. "We had to slow down a lot for fishermen, canoes, other boats and the jet skis that love to jump our wake," the Captain said. "They didn't realize we didn't have any breaks and it takes some distance to slow it down."

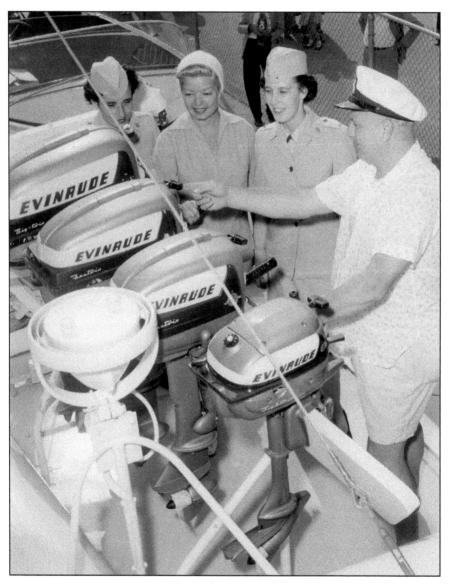

Frances visits the Evinrude factory.

Ralph and Frances get married.

The love birds sail away.

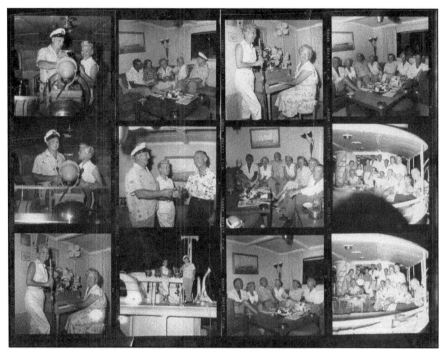

Entertaining aboard the *Chanticleer*.

How to get around a vast estate.

Frances and Ralph aboard the *Chanticleer*.

Frances and Ralph hobnob with celebrities John Forsythe and Art Linkletter in
the late '70s/early '80s.

Ralph Evinrude with his portrait of Frances Langford.

8   *Hand Still In*

FRANCES HAD PRETTY much retired from Hollywood by the mid-1950s. But not completely. When the RKO Unique record label asked her for some songs, she couldn't refuse. She recorded "When You Speak with Your Eyes" and "Rocking in the Rocket Room" in late 1956.

In December of that same year it was reported that Charles Wick had signed Frances to a series of 10 half-hour "telefilms" for his Splendex Enterprises, sporting a take home pay of $340,000 for her. Filming would begin on January 8th. David Rose would furnish the music and MGM veteran Earl K. Brent would write special songs for her. Wick also told the press of a Broadway musical vehicle in the works for Frances.

Around this time Frances, Wick and Ralph Evinrude began a collaborative venture for television which they called Chanford Productions, which they owned jointly. Hedda Hopper, in her powerful newspaper column, wrote of one 1962 production which would star Ginger Rogers as a mom with a teenage daughter in *Husband and Wife*. Wick would produce the series, and Frances was set to play the best friend. But none of the Wick notions seemed to have panned out.

After a six-year absence from television, Frances returned. She still did a few NBC specials, such as the hour-long *Frances Langford Presents*, broadcast on March 15, 1959. Ralph didn't mind her working. But she didn't wholly like it. "I didn't like nightclubs. Everybody was always drinking and the atmosphere wasn't always nice."

IN MID-NOVEMBER OF 1966 Frances left on a tour of Vietnam with the USO Overseas Committee to entertain the troops. Tony Romano, Patty Thomas and Johnny Cuzzins rounded out the foursome, and Bob Hope joined them at some point. Frances told the press, "Oh, I suppose there might be a few of the older officers who will remember me." But Ralph wasn't too keen on his wife going into a war zone again.

"Not long ago," she explained, "Ralph and I were watching TV sets in different rooms of our home in Stuart. Martha Raye, who entertained fighting men in World War II and who is doing such fine work again in Vietnam, was being interviewed.

"I knew Ralph wasn't too keen on my going, because I had broached the subject several times. But as I walked into his room, he threw up his hands and said, 'I know, I know, you're going.'

"I've been working out in our gymnasium, swimming and sitting in that sweat-box for an hour every day."

The tour was to be completed on December 1st, at which time she would travel to the Philippines and meet Ralph in Manila, where he had some business to attend to. He wasn't going to tag along to 'Nam because, as he said, "The boys don't want a husband around—I know that." It was probably just as well, since, as Frances stated, when it came to clothes, "The USO said 'slinky, but light and non-wrinkling.'

"Bob Hope came to visit us in our Milwaukee place and was delighted that I was going over again. He offered me the services of his writers to provide me with some jokes.

"I've had some close calls on these trips, but the rewards are worth every nervous twinge." She promised to sing some of her standards, as well as some rock-n-roll for the boys.

But when it came to talking about the boys—and the Vietnam war—Frances later said, "Anything to do with our troops, I can't talk about it, so I'd rather not. I've never been able to. It's just the strangest thing. I don't think people understand enough. There are things you have to do and there is a time to quit, too, but who knows when it is? I just feel that I do my job the best I can and do what I can do for my country, and it's not up to me to say what's right or what's wrong."

MEANWHILE, *THE BICKERSONS* were still showing up and wowing audiences who had never forgotten them. Don Ameche and Frances Langford, directed by creator Phil Rapp, recorded two very successful Columbia albums in front of live audiences: *The Bickersons*, released in November of 1961, and *The Bickersons Fight Back*, released in August, 1962. They were enormously popular (and are still selling and streaming today). They were *so* popular—garnishing a lot of radio airplay, and even being broadcast on airplanes—that a compilation album called *The Bickersons Rematch* was put out in 1971. The BMI royalty checks for radio play for Rapp were enormous and continued to pay out for years and years.

So it was hardly surprising during these ensuing years that Don, Frances and Phil collaborated on a seemingly endless series of radio commercials for various clients, such as General Motors, Easy Off and Coffee Rich. The following is one such unpublished script.

RADIO COPY

CLIENT   RICH PRODUCTS CORP.
                DATE   1/12/67 TIME   60 secs.

PRODUCT   COFFEE RICH

STATION
                BICKERSONS "CREEL"
PROGRAM
==

TIME

SOUND: RIPPLING STREAM. HOLD THROUGH COMMERCIAL

JOHN: Blanche, be perfectly still. I think I've got a bite.

BLANCHE: Don't hurt him, John.

JOHN: Oh for Pete's sake, it's only a trout, Blanche. And besides, how do you know if a fish is a him or her? Quick, open the creel.

BLANCHE: What's the creel?

JOHN: It's the wicker basket you're wearing over your shoulder.

BLANCHE: He won't fit in there. It's full of Coffee Rich.

JOHN: Coffee Rich!

BLANCHE: Yes. You know how you love it in your coffee every morning. You always say Coffee Rich tastes better than cream and brings out the full-bodied flavor of even my coffee.

JOHN: True.

BLANCHE: And you like the lively new flavor Coffee Rich gives to your morning cereal.

JOHN: I know, I know. And I like Coffee Rich on fruit too. But we didn't need a whole creel full. We're only going to be here three weeks.

BLANCHE: Well, Coffee Rich keeps three weeks in the refrigerator. And I'll use some to make a cream sauce for all the trout you catch. My mother gave me a recipe.

JOHN: Your mother...

BLANCHE: You never did like my mother, did you, John?

JOHN: Oh, for Pete's sake. Here, put the trout in your pocket and let's get back to the lodge.

ANNCR: That's Don Ameche and Frances Langford as the Bickersons. They agree on only one thing... Coffee Rich, the new non-diary creamer that tastes better than cream, costs less and with less calories, too. In pints or quarts. In your grocer's frozen food section.

At home in Jensen Beach.

9 *The Later Years*

IN 1971 *PALM BEACH LIFE* did a full-color spread on the happy couple in their Florida home. Entitled "Up a Lazy River," it showcased the Evinrude wealth lavishly and positively. Susannah Wood wrote of Perry Como and Vaughan Monroe and other famous Florida settlers dropping in at the Outrigger restaurant to croon out a number. Frances said, "They get it out of their systems. It's kind of nice because it's a homey place, and it's easy to sing because you've got a wonderful accompanist."

There were photos of Frances in her spacious living room with her poodles and feeding the wild peacocks on a wooden bridge. There were about 50 peacocks running wild on the estate, as well as geese and ducks, so sliding screen walls were constructed around the area, so the birds could live around the manmade lake, near a sulphur spring. Along with some undeveloped acreage, there was a small Kissimmee Swamp, on which Ralph built Frances a shack so that she might enjoy the wild birds. It was a swamp filled with foot paths and rounded, high-backed bridges.

Their main house was two stories, with the second floor teeming with floor-to-ceiling windows for sweeping views of the rolling hill leading to the St. Lucie River. Lacy grillwork framed the dining room entrance, with steps at the end of the living room leading to a comfortable bar. The walls were part panel, part brick. A long outside porch was an extension of the living room, covered with grass-like carpeting. The poodles didn't like to step on that part.

The His & Hers kitchen was set up with double cabinets for spices and a large collection of cookbooks. (I myself sent Frances a Chili Cookbook as a thank you gift for helping me with my Bickersons book, because I knew she loved making chili. She soon informed me she liked the book so much, she bought many copies of it for her friends.)

Guests were put in a different house, with a single, huge bedroom, with two baths, and it worked well.

Behind the living room was a gallery. At the time (1971), there were 65 Emile Gruppi canvases on the walls. The colorful pictures sometimes showed the Evinrudes and their friends on picnics and fishing trips.

The ground floor held offices, garages, utility areas, and Ralph's studio/office. Sometimes he would use this area to demonstrate or tinker with a new motor, machine or tank.

The grounds were so large that the Evinrudes and guests would often use golf course-like vehicles to get from one end to the other. There was also a big warehouse on the estate, where just about everything was kept, including a barrel organ that would crank out the famous tunes Frances was famous for.

THEY ALSO OWNED A RESTAURANT.

Ralph and Frances thought that their local harbor needed a place where sailors could get a sandwich and meal after they docked. Frances called it her "Polynesian paradise." Though it was a popular eating place on the Treasure Coast, "actually, the Outrigger was a hobby. The restaurant was a sort of break-even operation, but I had a gift shop that made money. We ended up making money for about 10 years." That was because word of mouth spread. "So we began adding on rooms."

"The first night, there was this long line outside the place, and we looked at each other and said, 'What is this?' People had decided that this was where they wanted to eat. So we started adding on rooms, then some guest houses.

"I'm not the regularly scheduled vocalist in the Outrigger, but yes, now and then they still do get me to sing."

In a pamphlet titled "A Brief History of the Outrigger Resort," the following description was given:

> Frances Langford fell in love with Jensen Beach after a visit here in the late 1930's. She purchased the land that is the Outrigger Resort in 1940. A row of villas was constructed on the west side of Indian River Drive, and a 400' long deck added into the beautiful Indian River.
>
> In 1943, the original marina was dredged, and "The Langford Villas and Marina" became a tourist resort, operated by James Langford, her brother.

During World War Two, as Frances Langford toured the South Pacific with the U.S.O., she dreamed of transforming her resort into a Polynesian paradise, duplicating the beauty, the floral colors, the exotic foods, exciting beverages, and the moods of the South Pacific.

It took the storybook romance of Frances Langford and Ralph Evinrude, that began one evening when they met as she was performing at Jimmy Fazio's Night Club in Milwaukee, resulting in marriage in 1955, to bring the dream to fruition.

Ralph Evinrude, being marine oriented, could appreciate the Polynesian dream. On a trip to Los Angeles, the Evinrudes met and talked with Ed Lawrence, a noted designer of Polynesian effects, set designer of the film *Rain*, and creator of the "Don the Beachcomber" restaurants. Lawrence agreed to assume the task of transporting Polynesia to Jensen Beach, Florida.

After five years of planning and design, during which the villas were expanded with duplexes and apartments to increase rental units, Lawrence created Frances Langford's Outrigger Resort and Restaurant. A gala opening was held during Christmas week of 1961.

With the resort complete, featuring 27 rental units and the 26 slip marina able to accommodate yachts up to 120 feet in length, the restaurant was the finishing touch.

Frances Langford's Outrigger Resort, ranked in 1984 as a Mobil three star property, is now nationally recognized and the restaurant (which also achieved a three star rating in its own right) is a landmark on the central east coast of Florida. The spacious villas with 1, 2, or 3 bedrooms are fully air conditioned and feature full-service kitchens. The facilities include a heated swimming pool, shuffleboard courts, deep-sea charter fishing boats and access to golf, tennis and numerous water sports nearby. The marina, which has an 8-foot draft at low tide, has hookups for electricity, water and cable TV and offers showers, laundry and refueling facilities.

The setting is unique on a point of land alongside the Outrigger Marina, with a spectacular view of the Indian River.

The best description of Ed Lawrence's creation of the Outrigger Restaurant is contained in Nixon Smiley's book, *On the Beat, and Offbeat* (Banyan Books, Miami, FL):

"Of all the restaurants Lawrence has built (including Don the Beachcomber of Hollywood and Chicago), he is proudest of the Outrigger.

"To age wood... make it look centuries old... he used an automobile fender grinder. The wood was then burned black with the aid of a gas torch, after which a steel brush was used to emphasize the patterns of the grain...

"Building materials included bamboo, rattan, woven palm matting, pecky cypress, straw and palm fronds, all fireproofed. Rafters and other structural members were reinforced by steel as needed, but all such construction was hidden. Even bolts were countersunk and covered by dowels.

"Gabel ends of the Outrigger are of plastic, embedded with sea shells, fan coral, pieces of old fish netting, and other 'treasures' one might expect to find washed up on the seashore. Fantastic effects are obtained by playing lights through the transparent plastic.

"Props to complete the Polynesian atmosphere include glass net floats, tapa cloth, and anything from the sea or seashore that seems to fit. An Outrigger canoe hangs among the heavy ceiling timbers (properly outfitted with a small Evinrude outboard engine). The scene, wherever one looks, might have been lifted from Pago Pago, and transported to Jensen Beach. That the 'set' is strictly fictional makes not the slightest difference that the food preparation is of Chinese origin rather than Polynesian.

"Fiction, of course, can be among the greatest of the arts, whether in the form of a novel like *Rain* or in the form of a Polynesian restaurant made of Hollywood materials and 'Polynesian food' cooked in woks by Chinese chefs. In the kitchen, the fiction stops."

In Frances Langford's Outrigger Restaurant and Resort, the dream has come true... the Polynesian paradise imagined by Frances Langford, star of stage, screen, television, and entertainer overseas in three wars, and the Cinderella marriage and partnership of Miss Langford and Ralph Evinrude, made it all happen.

Welcome to Frances Langford's Outrigger Resort, a dream built on love.

Frances sold the restaurant in 1983 to Fred Ayers who paid $1.5 million for it. He renovated it and called it the Dolphin Bar and Shrimp House. Frances attended the opening night. The 250-seat restaurant sports movie posters and photos of Frances to this day.

FRANCES ENJOYED GOOD HEALTH in her later years, but by March of 1978 she had to have open heart surgery at the Miami Heart Institute. She pulled through fine. It did not stifle her traveling or activity one bit and soon she and Ralph were back on board the yacht. They also took trips to the Philippines where Ralph had an engineering plant.

In October of 1982 Frances sang the national anthem for a Milwaukee Brewer's game. "It is a little difficult to sing," she said in an interview before the appearance, "because the range is so wide and the lyrics are a little difficult. But I don't anticipate any trouble. I'll just go down to the ball park a couple of hours before game time and speak to the organist, Frank Charles, about how we'll do it. We probably won't even rehearse." She eagerly looked forward to singing it. "It's the thought behind it that thrills you."

Ralph owned the team, and it was the team's first World Series. It was also Frances' first time singing the national anthem at a baseball game. "I told Ralph years ago," she said, "if these guys ever get to the World Series, I'll sing the national anthem. But I said by then I'll probably be in a wheelchair. But, oh God, what my worry is, if I ever forget the lyrics, I'll just end it all right there!"

RALPH DIED IN MAY OF 1986. It was a difficult time for Frances. She sold their Fox Point, Wisconsin home and remained living in Florida full time.

Even after Ralph was gone, Frances continued to make her yearly pilgrimages to that little Canadian cabin, on her 45-foot Norseman sport fisherman, the *Fran E*. She kept a crew of six, traveling with her best friend Patty Thomas. "That's where we have most of our fun: on board," Frances said of her travels. "When I'm on a trip I don't want to come home, and vice versa. It's kind of crazy." She still fished; better than a lot of *men*. "Women bring them in easily, even with the 20-pound test line. They don't just jerk them in the way men tend to. It's all about finesse."

Her last performing credit was for the 1989 PBS documentary, *Entertaining the Troops*. Frances sang "It's Been a Long Long Time" to open the program which was a lovely and positive reunion with Bob Hope, Patty Thomas and Tony Romano. They traded stories about Hope getting fungus on his feet and Frances getting fungus in her ear. Frances ended the program by singing her standard, "I'm in the Mood for Love." It was the perfect adieu to a happy career.

ON NOVEMBER 18, 1994 Frances married Harold Stuart, Assistant Secretary of the Air Force under Harry Truman, and also under Stuart Symington, who was famous in his own right. Stuart was by then an attorney in Tulsa, Oklahoma. Bob and Dolores Hope attended the ceremony on Hutchinson Island, and Patty Thomas was her Matron of Honor. They also spent summers on their Georgian Island in Canada, traveling from Florida on their yacht. "The mountains are all around," she said. "If you've ever seen fjords, that's what this looks like. I've been going there for 45 years."

She and Harold donated hundreds of acres of land for Langford Park in Jensen Beach, Florida, and created a garden on the corner of Palmer Road and Dixie Highway.

Kim Stanton states, "Frances and her third husband, Harold C. Stuart, placed an ad in our local paper for a personal assistant. I applied for the job which only listed a fax number. They called me the same day for an interview. We all hit it off from the start because, I, being a native Floridian and a nature-lover, and Mr. and Mrs. Stuart, had a lot in common. As a little girl, my friend, Vicki Knight, and I would visit the Frances Langford Resort. You see, my friend's father, Bill Knight, worked for Frances so we were allowed to swim in the resort pool and wander around the marina. She was the local celebrity and I told these stories to Mr. and Mrs. Stuart during the interview. We laughed together a lot during that interview. The next day I was told I had the job. It really was a dream position; to be associated with such wonderful, warm and caring people. They allowed me to work around my children's schedule who were 9 and 11 at the time.

"I worked for her in her home as her personal assistant from 1998 until she died at 92 in 2005. I read her mail to her and we answered her fan mail together. We would have fund raising parties on her yacht and on her estate down at what she called the Hut, which was a replica of a Polynesian Village type of hut designed by a Hollywood set designer.

"I knew Harold C. Stuart very well too as he and I did a lot of work together, i.e. writing letters, planning, contacting friends, Christmas gift giving orders, charity events, publicity, etc. He was a wonderful man.

Very involved in the local community—Boy Scouts, Ducks Unlimited, his alma mater University of Virginia, and, of course, Tulsa, Oklahoma. He had many, many friends and was quite active. He loved fishing, hunting, traveling, history and keeping in touch with his friends. Most of all, his main goal in life was to make Frances happy and be and enjoy her."

FRANCES WAS IN THE NEWS again in June of 2001 when she gained the support of her neighbors to fight back against the police's request that Frances should do something about the one hundred peacocks that roamed her estate. The county gave her a choice: either move them off the estate, or clip their wings and build a big fence.

In late 2002, Frances was inducted into the State Women's Hall of Fame by Governor Jeb Bush. Her name will forever be displayed on the plaza level of the Florida state Capitol. Though she wasn't able to attend due to her husband's illness.

Her awards were plentiful because her charity work never stopped; there were *many* newspaper articles giving credit where credit was due. She donated to the Hibiscus Children's Center, the American Red Cross, Hospice of Martin & St. Lucie, Martin Memorial Foundation, the Salvation Army, the Boy Scouts of America, and on and on. She had purchased band uniforms for Martin County High School for at least 15 years. She donated money for the Jensen Beach Causeway, and donated land for a public park in Jensen Beach, on which she built the Log Cabin Senior Center for clients of the County on Aging of Martin County. She made her *Chanticleer* available to the United Way of Martin County's Alexis de Tocqueville Society for their annual fund raiser, as well as to the clergy for their annual Blessing of the Fleet.

Kim Stanton added, "These are just a few of the hundreds of charities in our community that the Frances Langford Foundation has helped over the years: Alzheimer's Community Care, American Red Cross, Big Brothers Big Sisters, Big Heart Brigade (feeding the hungry with Thanksgiving Day dinners), Boys & Girls Clubs of Martin County, Caring Children Clothing Children, Castle, Children's Museum of the Treasure Coast, Council on Aging of Martin County, The Kane Center, Florida Arts & Dance Company, Florida Oceanographic Society, Helping People Succeed, Hibiscus Children's Center, Historical Society of Martin County, House of Hope, Humane Society of the Treasure Coast, Life Builders of the Treasure Coast, Light of the World Charities, Mary's Shelter of the

Treasure Coast, Molly's House, New Horizons, Pink Tie Friends, Project Graduation Foundation, Safe Space, Samaritan House of Boys, Treasure Coast Hospices, Volunteers in Medicine, and Whole Child Connection. She was also a major donor to our local hospital, Martin Memorial."

Nancy Smith, Associate Editor of *The Stuart News* wrote, "I was aboard the *Chanticleer* during the Blessing of the Fleet in 1997. It was enormously impressive. On each boat that passed along the starboard side, crews stood silent, heads lowered, while three robed clergymen in the bow of the *Chanticleer* said a prayer or made the sign of the cross. Frances told me at the time, 'I do this because I like to. It's only a little thing, but it's something I can give back to the community.'

"Well, no, it isn't 'only a little thing.' For the people of Martin and St. Lucie, especially the boaters among us, and the traditionalists like me who cherish such ceremonies, the generosity of Frances Langford Stuart is a very big thing."

A few times a year she even welcomed guests into her home for charity balls. One of the last ones was a "Swashbuckler" event for the Florida Oceanographic Society in which more than 600 guests attended. "If people don't know about me, well, that's okay," she said. "It doesn't matter. I still get fan mail from the movies I did, and those people still think I'm 18 years old, and they want a picture. I don't send them a picture of me today. I send them one maybe about five or six years ago or something. I'm 91 and I feel like I'm about 41."

"She was always busy," Kim explained, "always active—right up until she died, planning parties, making appearances. I would have to go with her and she would trust me to set up interviews with folks who wanted to interview her.

"Her biggest project was a family Christmas party every year. She would have all kinds of ideas about shopping for gifts. She did it herself for many years and I helped her toward the end. She would wrap every gift. She was a lovely person.

"Every summer she would travel on her yacht to her home in Canada. In order to prepare for that trip, there was always a lot of planning and activity. The crew would need the proper documents and her two dogs would have to have the proper vaccinations and documents. There were a myriad of things to do.

"I have known Frances to have Great Danes, an Alaskan Husky, but mostly poodles. She loved white poodles. When I came to work for her, she had Beau, a miniature poodle who was less than one year old. Beau ended up being a little larger than a mini and she always joked about that. She also joked that he 'failed sandbox' because he went in for house training, but he didn't quite hit the mark, if you know what I mean. Beau went to live with Patty Thomas, Frances' long time best friend and companion, out in Newport Beach, California, after Frances died. She also owned a Maltese at the time of her death, Sunny Boy. He went to live with Patty, too.

"Frances loved animals of all kinds. She owned chickens and ducks. She fed the local peacocks every day. When she traveled, it was the responsibly of the staff to make sure the peacocks were fed. She owned a cat at the time of her death, Miss Kitty. Miss Kitty stayed home when she traveled.

"She was singing up to just a few months before she died. She stood up on a balcony and sang at the local Indian Riverside Park here. She was still beautiful."

ON JANUARY 7, 2003 Larry King wrote to Frances to ask her to contribute to his new book, *Remember Me When I Am Gone*, "a collection of eulogies and epitaphs written by well-known people from all walks of life, as they would like to be remembered." He'd already collected epitaphs from Dave Barry, Stephen King, Bob Dole, Calvin Klein and over 20 others. Frances responded by writing, "It is a great idea for a book and coming from you, I know that it will be first-rate." And she included the following, fitting statement:

> Please remember me as a simple person, who loved this country,
> its people and especially its military servicemen and women.
> Our servicemen needed us, and we were there. I will always
> consider it one of the greatest honors of my life to entertain
> the troops during the war years with Bob Hope and the U.S.O.

FRANCES LANGFORD DIED IN 2005 of congestive heart failure at her Jensen Beach home. Condolences poured in from celebrities and fans alike. She lived such a full and giving life, and will never be forgotten, not as a performer nor as a humanitarian. And it's with a touch of sadness to say that her kind—so talented, so beautiful, so generous—is so rare, that we may never see it again.

Frances, Ralph and Ed Lawrence, architect of The Outrigger, outside the restaurant.

At the Falcon Foundation, November 3, 1989, with Dolores Hope.

Frances and her 105 lb. Tarpon caught by Frances at Boca Grande, Florida.

Unknown man, Frances and Stuart on board the *Chanticleer* on one of their summer trips to Canada.

Dining with Bob Hope in The Outrigger.

Frances and Stuart pose for their 1998 Christmas card photo with Beau, their poodle. Taken in "The Hut," a Polynesian style outbuilding on the estate.

APPENDIX 1

Letters

ON DECEMBER 21, 2001, television broadcaster Hugh Downs wrote to Frances: "The catastrophic events of September 11, 2001 have left all Americans shaken and stirred. I am writing you and a number of other prominent Americans to ask for your participation, which will surely help to give the book the high profile it deserves. I am asking you to write a brief statement of 100-400 words or so, describing how you view our country in this time of heightened awareness and concern." The book had a publication date of September 11, 2002—the first anniversary of the tragedy. A portion of the book's proceeds would be donated to UNICEF, and each participant received either $100 or that amount sent to their favorite charity. The 150 contributors included current performers, and past and current celebrities, such as John Glenn, Paul Harvey, George Bush, Alan Alda and Paul Simon. The deadline for participation in the Simon & Schuster book was January 28, 2002. *My America: What My Country Means to Me, by 150 Americans from All Walks of Life* is still in print.

January 14, 2002

Dear Hugh,

I received your letter of December 21, 2001 and want to commend you on such a fine project. I knew right away that I would like to participate and be a part of your creation. Per your specific request, below is my statement describing how I view our country. Let me know of your progress with the book.

My America, What My Country Means To Me

When Hugh first asked me to give a brief statement on what my country means to me personally, I pondered this big subject with a sense of awesomeness. I had thoughts of so many things to share in light of recent events on September 11th and considering all I have seen and done in my own life. I will try to put into words my heartfelt beliefs and how they relate to this wonderful country we call home—The United States of America.

I love The USA and the spirit of this country that is reflected by the American people. That fortitude is represented in many different ways, but I am especially interested in, drawn to and appreciative of our courageous military men and women. To believe in America means to believe in freedom, peace, equality, and justice—among many other attributes. To deem these certain aspects of decency important enough to fight for and possibly die for is the ultimate service and can only aide in the continued promise of these American ideals. That is why I chose to serve our young soldiers during World War II, along with Bob Hope and many others, in the best way that I knew how—entertainment! Looking into the eyes of our young GIs and singing to them before they headed off to battle, visiting wounded soldiers in makeshift hospitals and just trying to bring some smiles from home to our boys was one of the greatest honors and the greatest sadness for me—it was truly bittersweet. I was so drawn to help in some way for the cause of freedom because I love this country and everything we represent.

My America and what my country means to me can be summed up by something a true American once said about this country—"In all, it is a great country. It's the best and the worst one I ever lived in, and I been living in countries for fifty-four years next November fourth."—Will Rogers.

Sure, we have a lot of problems in the good ole' U.S. of A— you must take the bad with the good, constantly working on the ills of society to make an even better America. The bottom line for me is we live in the greatest country on earth.

– Frances Langford
01/14/02

Hugh, I wish you much success in putting this book together. If you make any changes due to length restrictions, etc. please inform me or fax a draft for my approval. Hopefully your attempts to create a diversified volume will be met. It has been a trip down memory lane for me and very difficult to talk and think about at times... Thank you for the invitation to participate.

Sincerely,
Frances Langford

October 29, 2001

Jeb Bush, Governor of the State of Florida
Executive Office
Tallahassee, Florida

Dear Governor Bush,

I was pleased to receive your complimentary 4th of July letter as we celebrated Independence Day this year. I send my apologies for not replying sooner. We are only now returning by boat from a long vacation in Canada.

Our cabin, which is on a small island in Canada, is called "home" every year at this time, for about a month. The fishing, perfect climate and good company are very inviting. One month is spent on the waterways, en route to the cabin and, of course, another final month back to Florida. As wonderful as these vacations are, some of the best and lasting memories I have were with Bob Hope as we served by performing with the USO Tours during WWII, Korea and Vietnam. This year in Canada is one we will not forget because of the great tragedy that has befallen our nation.

Now, it is my turn to send praises to you for a "job well done" as you govern this great state and especially at this trying time. We stand united with you and your brother, our President, George W. Bush. Continued leadership, strength and resolve is our wish for you and your entire family.

I was not expecting such nice accolades from our Governor. I want you to know how much it meant to me to receive your letter during the 4th of July and it means even more now. Thank you for your devotion to the State of Florida and to the causes of liberty and freedom!

Sincerely,
Frances Langford

From *2nd Marine Division Assoc. Magazine*, March/April 2002

Frances Langford, Angel on Earth
by E. R. McElveen (G-2-6)

It was 1944. I was wounded on June 15 at Red Beach One on Saipan and again on June 27 when I was evacuated to a Radio Station Field Hospital on Saipan. After five days I was evacuated again to the *U.S.S. Bountiful* Hospital Ship, from which I was put off at Tulagi Island in the Solomons at a Naval Hospital. There, I began to recuperate from a gunshot wound to the upper body and lung.

We were all weak from our experience and walked very slowly around the hospital grounds—when we could walk at all. At this time we were told that there would be a program featuring Bob Hope at the local naval base and that we could go, as trucks would be sent to pick up the walking wounded. I was just getting out of bed a little, but I wanted to see Bob Hope. So, the doctor agreed to let me try to make the trip.

Those of us who could walk got on a truck, which transported us to the site of the program. There, we were entertained by Hope and his entourage of pretty girls and comedians. From there, we were returned to our own ward at the hospital. Soon, a jeep drove up to our ward. A few people got out and came into our ward, which consisted of a long canvas top over a wooden floored frame.

One of the people who came in was Frances Langford. She sang a few songs for us, which we enjoyed very much. She was told that there were four Marines at the end of the ward who had gangrene and had but a few days to live. The odor of these men was so bad that anyone who went into the area would be likely to throw up. Some of the Corpsmen who went into the area did just that.

Frances Langford walked right into the area where they were and started talking to them. She went over and kissed each one, and asked what they would like her to sing. Without any music or backup, she sang a song for each of them. If I ever heard an angel sing, she was that angel. Then she went by and kissed each one of them again. There was not a dry eye in that whole field hospital ward.

Is there a place in the Marine Corps where she will always be remembered? I, for one, will always speak her name with reverence.

APPENDIX 2
Selected Purple Heart Diary Columns

Cincinnati, Feb. 25—Rehabilitation for the tubercular veteran has always been close to my heart.

So I am very happy to pass along to you some information on this subject contained in a letter from Edward Hochhauser, executive director of the committee for the Care of the Jewish Tuberculous, Incorporated.

Writing me from New York, Mr. Hochhauser stated:

"I was very much interested in your recent article discussing the tuberculous veteran.

"We have been supplying the kind of service which you so properly point out is necessary in restoring the tuberculous veteran and civilian to his place as a normal, self-sustaining person. We have operated a sheltered workshop, with supplementary medical, social economic and, where necessary, psychiatric services.

"The results have shown that seen moderately or far advanced cases who cure successfully at the hospital and go through the kind of services that we provide, have the normal life expectancy of men and women of their own age.

"Recently we started a new service at our workshop which provides the cardiac patient with the same services.

"We need to repeat that the readjusted tuberculous patient makes a satisfactory employee, and unless the man who has been prepared has a chance to work, he becomes a disgruntled and unhappy person, with the chances of relapse very high indeed."

I'm sure Mr. Hochhauser would have his motion emphatically seconded by many of the TB boys who have personally recounted to me their job-hunting misadventures.

More organizations like Mr. Hochhauser's are vitally needed. Arrested TB cases can never regain productive citizenship on a permanent basis unless we give them the right kind of chance to do so.

[Undated] The other day we went to Canada to open their sixth war loan drive and while there entertained at several hospitals. I was a little shocked to hear of so many Canadian casualties as I had sort of forgotten Canada has been fighting in this war for five long years.

You don't hear a great deal about what the Canadian boys are doing but they also know the meaning of the Purple Heart. You only have to visit their many hospitals to realize that.

I sang to boys without arms or legs, boys in wheelchairs and on stretchers, and boys in casts from their heads down to their feet.

When I walked into the first ward and saw all those boys gathered there I got a lump in my throat as big as an egg. I didn't think I would be able to sing or talk. But as I stood for a second and looked at they wanted and that's what they wanted and that's what they were going to get.

When I finished singing, I noticed a nurse coming towards me leading a soldier carrying a bunch of roses. He presented them to me and said they were just a token of appreciation, not only from the boys there but from all the wounded boys I had ever sung for.

I can't explain the feeling I had in my heart at that moment.

The soldier was not more than 18 years old. He was blind in both eyes and his right arm was gone.

It's things like that that make one feel no matter how much we are doing, it's still too little.

VANCOUVER, B. C., March 12 (AP)—The Royal Canadian Air Force in co-operation with the Canadian Pacific Air Lines has agreed to provide an aircraft to a woman prepared to spend her $3500 savings in a dream-inspired search for her missing aviator-husband.

The plane will be provided for Mrs. Marjorie Ramsay, Toronto, to search for her husband. Flight Lt. George Ramsay, who was aboard an RCAF flying boat that has been missing three months, Air Vice Marshal

F. V. Heakes, chief of the RCAF Western Air Command, announced tonight.

Mrs. Ramsay said she had a dream about a "Kent Island" and was prepared to spend all of her savings searching the area of Kent Island, about 265 air miles northwest of Vancouver. Air force officials said the area had been searched thoroughly by land, sea and air on two occasions since Ramsay's flying boat disappeared.

PALM SPRINGS, Cal., Oct. 13.—When 2nd Lt. Carroll Jones, Jr., of New York, was first admitted to Torney General Hospital here as a patient, he was a pretty melancholy individual. He had to struggle against a full load of depression. Even his art work was unattractive to him.

But morale oftimes turns on small things for our hospitalized veterans. In Lt. Jones' case it was the sublime courage and sunny disposition of a little Chinese, 23-year-old Pvt. Don Fong, of San Francisco, that did the trick.

While I was visiting another boy's cot, Fong shyly approached Patty Thomas, who had accompanied me to Torney to give the boys a dancing treat, and politely requested:

"Please tell Miss Langford I heard her sing in Sicily. Maybe she'll talk to me."

Miss Thomas graciously introduced us and I learned that Fong was among the 19,000 battle-weary men I had entertained from a captured Nazi tank in an open Sicilian gully.

WOUNDED IN ITALY.

Fong came out of that campaign okay, but he didn't fare so well in Italy.

Nazi shrapnel plowed through his elbow and tore gaping holes in his stomach. He was flown to Torney for a very complicated operation. Bad as his condition was, his first thought was of his parents in far-off free China. They must be spared the agonizing news of his serious wounds, was his earnest request. Hospital authorities humanely withheld the information from them.

Then Col. M. G. Beaver, formerly of Mayo Clinic, went to work. The operation he had to perform was extremely difficult. It called for the closing of extensive abdominal wounds. Battle-field surgeons had left them open to avoid infection.

But first Fong had to be prepared for the ordeal. While awaiting his operation Fong was one of the cheeriest patients in the hospital. His friendly smile and good humor were a tonic for other convalescing heroes at Torney. He soon became the pet of the institution.

SKETCHED OPERATION.

Among those who fell under Fong's spell was Lt. Jones. When Fong went into the operating room Jones was with him. While Col. Beaver worked with his instruments Jones worked with a pencil and drawing board. Each step in Col. Beaver's intricate operation became a permanent record via Jones' drawing, which later were converted from black and white drawing into color paintings.

The Fongs in China now know that their Don underwent a successful operation; that he will be as good as new in a few weeks and able to return to battle action.

Jones is definitely out of the black water and into a permanent assignment of sketching other intricate operations as ward administrator to the surgical service branch. For his paintings are a real contribution to medicine. Through him even recently graduated medical officers can be taught Col. Beaver's successful technique.

But the fruitful consequences of Fong's morale-boosting spirit hasn't stopped there.

By an odd coincidence, officers of the Hollywood Chapter No. 83. Military Order of the Purple Heart, were present at Torney during my visit. They told me of the important road in clinical study opened by Jones' paintings. I'll tell you about this road in my next article.

PALM SPRINGS, Cal., Oct. 23.

OCCUPATIONAL therapy is playing a great part in the lives of convalescent heroes here at Torney General Hospital. During my recent visit I was fortunate enough to be taken through the O. T. ward where Miss Rose Cezer, departmental head, and her assistant, Miss Ila Johnson, showed me how occupational therapy works.

Technically it's a prescribed treatment therapeutically applied. In terms of human relationship, it means the all-important bridge back to normal life for hundreds of wounded GI Joes. Meticulous care in fitting the activity to the man is the core of O. T. No stone is left unturned in placing him where is his injured part can function as normally as possible.

I'm happy to say it's working with a capital W.

Let's meet one of the boys currently absorbing its benefits. There's Corp. George P. Georgian, for example. Corp. Georgian, a purple heart wearer, is a Los Angeles boy. He lived at 1014 E. 82d St. before he went olive drab.

NINETEEN-YEAR-OLD and an infantryman, Corp. Georgian was starting his second year in service when it happened. A Nazi 88 mm shell kayoed him during our momentous invasion of Normandy. Fragments from the shell ripped into his right leg and right arm, causing multiple fractures in the latter member.

As soon as the casts were off, doctors at Torney prescribed O. T.'s pattern-weaving loom.

"Working that loom." Georgian told me, "was the greatest medicine in the world for me. At first my arm was still as a board. I thought I'd never be able to raise it. The first time I tried to the pain was so awful I saw stars."

To Georgian that pain was a greater enemy than the Nazis could ever hope to be. But leave it to the American doughboy to surmount any difficulty. Inch by inch he began to raise that pain-wracked arm. Finally he was able to lift it high enough to straighten thread.

THEN began the second stage of his fight: moving the loom's shuttle and beating the thread. A new set of pains beset him. On he kept, though, gradually licking it. Now he's graduated from the loom and is ready for something more interesting in woodwork or plastics.

We, on the outside cannot begin to realize the deep obligation we owe to men like Georgian. There's a simple way for us to offer at least token payment.

While O. T. is specifically medical, it often points the way and opens up a new field professionally to some chap whose disability has taken his former vocation away from him.

Now Uncle Sam cannot always supply the materials that may enable these men to be on their own again. That's where you and I come into the picture.

ALL of us may well follow the lead of the Los Angeles chapter of the Communications Corps of the United States. The human dynamo commanding this outfit, Maj. Mabel E. Patton, cousin of Lt.-Gen. George S. Patton, and her co-workers have secured Torney a fully-equipped work bench for jewelry and art metal making.

But the O. T. shop can use other things. Metal work files of all kinds. Tooling calf leather measuring a minimum of 4 x 9 in. A leather punch to drill holes for the wallets the men make. And at least 12 tables vises, 2½ to 2¾ inches or larger, for metal, plastic and wood work.

CORONO, Cal., Oct. 30.

MY VISIT to the U.S. Naval Hospital here was an unexpected and heartwarming surprise.

The moment our party, including Patty Thomas, the dancer, and members of the Communications Corps of Los Angeles, stepped into its spacious corridors and saw the fellows lined up, all grinning their broadest as members of the roving reception committee, we sensed the morale in the hospital was Four Point O (Navy for tops).

I had expected something quite different. The wards at Norco (it used to be the Norconian Country Club) are filled with victims of one of man's most deadly and baffling diseases—rheumatic fever. A disease that medical science knows, but few parents realize, is the arch killer of children. It murders one of every eight children and young grownups who die from the disease. It is many times more prevalent and fatal in children than infantile paralysis.

WARDS ARE CHEERUL.

Yet the rheumatic fever wards at Norco seem more like a haven than a hospital. Here is real cheerfulness. The inspiring atmosphere is of determined faith. Not a long face in a ward-load. Not an ounce of grimness.

The answer was quickly forthcoming from the lips of Capt. Lynn N. Hart, executive officer of the hospital, who conducted me through acres of wards especially constructed to permit sunshine at all hours. There is bad news ahead for the rheumatic terror. The Medical Corps of the Navy has made some progress and is making every effort to combat this insidious malady.

VEIL IS LIFTING.

Thanks to them, the veil of mystery shrouding rheumatic fever for 600 years is beginning to lift. Parents and victims of the disease can, at last, look hopefully to the future. A hope based not on wishful thinking alone but on the solid fact that 85 TO 90 PER CENT of the cases at Norco are returning to active service.

It is this hope that makes you think you're talking to Marine Pvt. Clarence R. Sewell in his Jeffersonville, Ind. workshop, instead of alongside his hospital cot.

Pvt. Sewell is eagerly looking forward to climbing back into his uniform. Proudly showing me the beautiful model plane he had made, he philosophically remarked:

"If it wasn't for my cat fever (Navy term for rheumatic fever), I wouldn't have been able to make this plane. I'm not so bad off at that."

DEEP FAITH IN MEDICS.

It is this hope also that causes Apprentice Seaman William Lee, Jennings, La., to grin so engagingly at me, with his black eyes dancing and dark hands beating a jive rhythm on the counterpane, as I stop at his private cubicle to say hello.

Lee is still a 24-hour bed patient, but the deep faith he has in the Navy medicos, plus his unbeatable spirit, will carry this Negro lad well past his misfortune.

Outside of the expert medically prescribed convalescence developed here (I will tell you more about it in my next article) there is still no known cure for rheumatic fever. Strong clues are beginning to appear, however.

HEARS TWO THEORIES.

Lt. Cmdr. George C. Griffith, one of the nation's most outstanding authorities on the malady, told me at least two theories have been exploded at Norco:

1. That microbes are the assassins. Streptococcic infection pulls the trigger that sets off the rheumatic fever attack, but the ammunition is a poison called antigen which attacks tissues.
2. That its aftermath is primarily heart trouble. Navy doctors have found the poison often attacks the lungs, kidneys, brain and other vital parts in addition to the heart.

There's no gulf between convalescing GI's and home fronters. About all they ask of us is we back up their buddies on the war fronts.

Whenever any bitterness is on display it's generally well justified.

At Oak Knoll Naval Hospital here I saw a young, blonde, good-looking Marine who had lost his right arm. The stump of it dangled at his side.

You get used to sights like that at the hospitals. I might have passed him with just a cheery "hello" or maybe a sentimental song, but there was something about his eyes that got me. They looked as if they'd seen all the sadness there was in the world.

"Is there anything I can do for you?" I said.

He looked up at me with those searching blue eyes of his. I thought he'd surely ask me to sing his favorite song. Or that he'd pour out his heart and tell me about some girl he loved who hadn't come to visit him.

FEATHER MERCHANT.

But for the moment he wasn't thinking about any girl. He wasn't even thinking of his own loss.

"A fellow was here just a short time ago during visiting hours," he said. "A civilian. Feather merchants, we call 'em. Anyway, this 'feather merchant' had a friend in the hospital who'd been wounded. And I guess he was trying to cheer him up.

"The feather merchant said he thought the European war would be over soon. 'Whenever the European war ends, oh, boy, what a celebration we'll have all over the United States!' he went on. 'Why, the armistice celebration after the last war won't even begin to compare with it. This'll be a riot. Everybody will get roaring drunk. The day will be a real national holiday. Personally, I'm saving my best Scotch for that day. If you're out of here by then, brother, we can both get drunk.'

"I guess the feather merchant meant well. He thought his friend and I would feel the same way about it as he did.

"Well, we don't. You can guess why, Miss Langford."

Yes, I could guess why. I knew this boy had fought in the South Pacific and that he had a kid brother still fighting in the steaming, Jap-infested jungles there.

He was afraid that on V-day—the day battles end in Europe—some defense workers might lay down their tools. While at the same time, thousands of miles away, Jap bullets would still be aimed at American boys.

When V-day comes American boys will still be munching K rations, alerted for Jap snipers in the thick foliage only yards away. B-29s will still be flying over Jap islands, and American boys in them will still be trying to destroy the little yellow sons of hell. And some of our own boys won't return.

HOW TO CELEBRATE.

"Well, you know how people are," I said to the boy who lay, pale and exhausted in his hospital bed. "They'll want to do something to show how glad they are one phase of the war is over."

He nodded his head.

"Sure, I know." he said. "Will you do something for me?"

I said I'd try, if it was humanly possible.

"Write an article, Frances, telling them what I and the other fellows here think. Tell them if they want to celebrate V-Day they should. But not by getting drunk and rioting in the streets. That week every individual on the home front should work an extra hour, buy an extra war bond or go to the blood bank to make a donation. Then he'll really be celebrating V-Day and making the day of final victory in the war come that much closer."

Okay, Marine, I think you're right. Will every man and woman who reads this decide to celebrate V-Day in the way that Marine said it should be celebrated? Will you make that pledge to me and to your country now? I'll be waiting to hear from you.

SAN DIEGO, Cal., Dec. 1.

SOME people feel that GI Joe will be so glad to shed khaki he'll forget what he's been fighting for. These professional worriers should stop kidding themselves.

Necessary military discipline has kept our fighting men subdued and restrained. But don't delude yourself into thinking that the traditional Yankee crusading spirit has flown the coop. Your average serviceman's pent-up demand for expressing himself is bound to burst forth like a raging torrent once he gets his discharge papers.

Pfc. William Thompson Adams, a Marine infantryman, is a good example. Adams, a native of Kansas City, Mo., didn't spend nearly two years in the South Pacific for nothing.

While helping the marines write history on Bougainville, Tarawa, Saipan, Tinian and finally Guam, Adams learned the American way of life is not just a slogan—it's a religion. This belief is in his blood—because blood on Guam was his tuition.

When I reached Adams' cot at the naval hospital here. I found him trying to comb his hair.

Self-conscious and apologetic, he earnestly explained:

"The nurse said you might pose for picture with me, Miss Langford. My cast keeps my head glued to this pillow and my hair's always mussed."

(Adams' entire right leg and torso is in a cast).

"Go right ahead and comb it," I said.

Although it will be weeks before Adams' cast will be removed, I noticed his uniform was where he could easily see it.

"That uniform means an awful lot to you," I observed.

"You bet it does, Frances," he proudly admitted. "Wearing it large. Never to take for granted what we have on this side of the drink.

"I never thought voting would be such a big deal in my life. It is now. Next to seeing June (his wife) and Suzzane (his 3-year-old daughter) I'm looking forward to voting."

"Do you mean in the next election?" I asked.

"No, in the last one." he said quite seriously. "I know the election's over for most people, but not for me. You see, my ballot hasn't caught up with me yet. I lost one of my best pals on Guam. My ballot—when it finally reaches me—is going to be cast in his memory."

The lump in my throat has taught me a great lesson: my heart beats for this display of Americanism. It's a pity our chicken-hearted alarmists couldn't have been within earshot. They'd never tell another soul our men don't know what they are fighting for.

A lady who signs herself, "A Lonesome Soldier's Wife" proudly sends in "For You," written to her by her soldier husband. Here are the first four lines:

FOR YOU
I do believe that God above Created you for me to love;
He picked you out of all the rest
Because he knew I loved you best!

ATLANTA, Ga., Dec. 22

TO MOST GI JOES a 30-day furlough is something about which to jump for joy. To Staff Sgt. George Wilson it is something that smacks of a nerve-wracking trial.

You have only to glance at Sgt. Wilson's boyish features, expressive brown eyes and blond tousled hair to realize that everything would turn out all right if he were the one on trial. But he isn't. It is John Q. Public who's on trial.

At 24 years of age Sgt. Wilson is a veteran of six years' service in the Army. He lived and worked on his father's farm at Henderson, N. C., before he joined the Army at 18.

When his outfit was called upon for the French invasion task, he became leader of his own squad.

LETTER HE DIDN'T WRITE.

"I thought what a nice thing it was going to be to write a letter from Paris to a certain young lady in Henderson," Wilson told me from his cot at Lawson General Hospital here. "I never got to write that letter, though. My buddy wrote her explaining why."

The explanation Wilson's sweetheart got was heart-breaking. Two Nazi shells scored direct hits on George as he was crawling toward a heavy artillery barrage from the enemy. His arm and leg were mangled. Shrapnel entered his right shoulder and four pieces penetrated his back and lodged in his chest.

At an aid station his leg and arm were amputated.

The wonders of rehabilitation performed by Army medical officers have helped bring light into darkness for him. During my visit he was gay and lighthearted.

WAITS ARTIFICIAL LIMBS.

"This goes double, Frances," he cracked as he put his one arm around me and hugged me in appreciation for the little entertainment I had given. "It won't be long now before I'll be able to hug you with two arms," he continued. "I'm getting an artificial arm and leg for my furlough."

"I'll bet you're looking forward to your furlough," I observed.

Wilson's face clouded up. "I'm not so sure about that," he gravely said. "I'm afraid I'll have a case of stage fright. Something like my dad's friend had when he started wearing his new toupee."

Wilson didn't say it, but plainly written on his face was the realization that his 30-day furlough was going to be the most crucial period of his life.

Wilson is frankly worried as to what kind of a reception is in store for him from homefronters. In France he dreamed about going home. Built it up in his mind to the point where it compared favorably with Paradise.

He's wondering now whether it's going to work out that way. It can— providing we spare no effort toward making him feel he's really home.

Re-learning to walk and to use his new arm is going to take many tedious hours. But it won't be half as tough as brooking morbid curiosity, over-solicitation, maudlin sentiment, tactlessness and encouragement of an invalid complex.

In Wilson's own words, being fitted out with a false leg and arm is going to make him "like new again." He won't feel that way unless you treat him as though he was new again!

VAN NUYS, Calif., April 20—Overseas our fighting men never stopped asking this question: Were they suckers for the sacrifices they were making?

I'll never forget the wistfulness of one such question. It was put to me by a tow-headed Yank in a Sicilian gully. He had just come out from under heavy fire. He bore the marks of battle. Torn uniform, battered helmet, dust and grime, all the rest of it.

"How are the home folks behaving?" he asked. "I sure hope they're taking care of things. All this is just no good if they don't give us decent treatment when we get back."

STILL ASKING IT IN HOSPITALS

Our hospitalized veterans are still asking that question. Only now the tone is less wistful. They are beginning to fear the worst. Disappointment and disillusionment are weighing them down. Being played for a sucker isn't something you can just laugh off.

Yet, here at Birmingham General Hospital, paralyzed veterans suffering from terrible spinal cord injuries, are jesting about it. It's a bitter jest, though.

"You know," they say, "your Purple Heart and a quarter will buy you a glass of beer."

They talk that way because of the many things that shadow their days and ways. But especially because of the shadows we helped to create and choose to ignore. The blackest of them all: Public Law 144.

The Hearst newspapers have exposed the evils of that law. Under it, ex-fighting men without dependents are deprived of their full disability pensions while undergoing care in Veterans' Administration hospitals. Their government (stingy to them alone) limits them to 68 cents a day if their disability is service-connected and 26 cents a day if it's not.

WORDS WITHOUT ACTION FUTILE

Military life taught these veterans respect for results. And results are what they are looking for. They are fed up with words without action, promises without fulfillment and soft sentimentality without paid bills.

They're not needling the Veterans' Administration about it. They know its officials who made Public Law 144; that they must do what the law says.

Ours is a country in which the people make the laws. We are the ones to decide what treatment our maimed and disabled vets will receive. So far our record is something to be ashamed of.

I don't think that in our hearts we meant to break faith with our defenders. Let's give them the results they're seeking—the results they so richly deserve. Let's restore their full disability pensions.

Put your Congressman to work righting a great wrong.

TOPEKA, Kas., Oct. 4—You treat wounded soldiers as they want to be treated.

A few are against the world. They look at you with hate.

They would look at anyone with hate who could walk.

You say "Hello" to them and leave them alone.

Then there are those who laugh the whole thing off. You adapt yourself to their mood.

Most of our returning wounded veterans are not bitter. They accept what happened to them as part of the necessary price of war.

You might think they would expect the rest of us, who have paid such a comparatively small price to keep America safe, to kowtow to them.

You might expect them to feel we owed them everything—as indeed we do. But that is not the way most of them feel.

In a hospital outside Chicago I passed one boy who had lost his left leg in the war. I passed him without saying more than just "Hello" because I thought perhaps the sight of a woman who was lucky enough to be able to walk might hurt him.

ASKED TO SING.

Then a young chap came running up to me.

"Gee," he said. "There's a guy who's dying to ask you to sing but he hasn't the nerve. Would you talk to him?"

I walked back into the ward and found that the boy who wanted me to sing was the one who had lost his leg.

"What would you like me to sing?" I asked.

The happy, half incredulous look on his face is a memory I will treasure forever.

"Do you mean," he said almost unbelievingly, "that you'll really sing for me?"

I told him that of course I would.

"Would it be all right if I sang 'Embraceable You?'"

WILL NEVER FORGET.

"That's for me," he said.

As I sang he went through all sorts of motions that he felt were in keeping with the song. He pretended to hug an imaginary girl.

When I finished he told me:

"This is a moment in my life I'll never forget."

He is about 18, very good-looking. You would think he would be very bitter lying there strapped to his bed. But that boy doesn't think the world owes him anything. He didn't even think I owed him a song.

I saw one boy who had been burned from head to toe. They had been trying to graft skin on him but it was very difficult.

His face had been fixed up but his arms and legs were like toothpicks. He said:

"My wife tells me she thinks I'm wonderful and as long as she thinks that, everything is all right."

And I think that as long as we show our wounded veterans that that is the way all of us feel about them everything will be all right in the long run.

PALM SPRINGS, Cal., Oct. 16.—In my previous article I related how a Chinese boy, Pvt. Don Fong of San Francisco, displaying the same indestructible spirit and unquenchable courage with which Mother China has stymied the Japs, has inspired an important contribution to medical science here at Torney General Hospital.

Fong's fortitude and pluck had won the admiration of 2d. Lt. Carroll Jones, Jr., and launched his technique-standardizing paintings. From his talented brush has blossomed the step-by-step progress of intricate operations performed at Torney, starting with the hazardous abdominal one successfully performed on Fong by Col. M. G. Beaver, formerly of Mayo Clinic.

Jones' paintings have proved very valuable to the staff in demonstrating the correct steps in operations for the closure of abdominal and other serious battle wounds.

ROOM FOR IMPROVEMENT.

However, Col. Beaver and Col. A. B. Jones, commanding officer of Torney, believe there is room for improvement; that even greater benefit can be derived from using color movies in conjunction with Lt. Jones' paintings.

The only thing stopping them is the little matter of financing it. Military hospitals are only allowed funds for barest necessities by the Government. Obtaining items like movie or still photographic equipment would require virtually a Congressional act. To the hapless staff, who are performing so many medical miracles for your disabled veterans, getting this equipment seems nothing but a dream.

It's a dream out of a twofold hope:

1. To ease the suffering and expedite the mending of casualties from every theatre of war.
2. To further the reconditioning program for those whose disabilities have taken them from the battlefield for good.

PHOTOGRAPHY AS TRADE.

In many cases those in the latter category will have to change vocations when they become civilians again. If the dream of the Torney staff comes true many could learn photography as a trade during convalescence.

It could also assist Torney's great plastic surgeon, Maj. Gilbert Hyroop, in giving Pfc. Earl M. Young, a North Carolina lad, at least part of one hand.

Young has made many trips to the excellently equipped operating room at Torney since he lost one hand and most of the other during maneuvers. Each time still photographs were taken, but without motion picture equipment, Maj. Hyroop was unable to study an invaluable pictorial record of the growing function of the hand.

Last week the cast on Young's hand was changed, offering Maj. Hyroop a golden opportunity of recording the movement of a new thumb, which with bone and pedicle grafts has been created through skillful surgery. Again he was stumped by lack of adequate photographic equipment.

VETERANS HELP OUT.

Into this breach has stepped an organization which is certainly living up to its name—the Hollywood Chapter No. 83, Military Order of the Purple Heart. They have tapped their modest treasury for $100 and started to make Torney's dream come true.

About $5,000 is needed for the various photographic items of equipment capable of providing color and black and white movies and stills for teaching surgical technique and new vocations for our convalescent heroes.

I, for one, will be very proud to join forces with the Purple Heart organization in advancing this most worthy project with my personal contribution. And if you could but see how earnestly and intensely everybody at Torney from Col. Jones down anticipates the motion picture equipment you would unhesitatingly join them too.

PALM SPRINGS, Cal., Oct. 18.

EVEN an occasional visitor to the fighting fronts finds it difficult to get readjusted to life at home. You see litters of freshly wounded Americans resting on mud one day. Then the next day a fast plane whisks you back to California; and you see that the land is dotted with victory gardens and ornamental flowers.

You see people who don't seem heartbroken because there's a war on. Children still play gaily on the streets. Everybody acts so normal, so natural.

So how can one blame Pvt. Stephen Louie, San Francisco Chinese, for thinking every day that dawns at Torney General Hospital is a miracle?

Just a few yards from the hospital gay vacationists are starting to flock to Palm Springs, heralding the opening of another season for this famous desert Winter playground. Movie stars and other celebrities are beginning to wander through its picturesque village.

A TRAGIC SCENE.

But at Torney the grim results of war stare at Pvt. Louie from every ward. He sees other wounded heroes strolling in the garden of what was once El Mirador Hotel, trying desperately to reorient themselves into the American scene.

After serving 13 months in western China with the American "Y" forces, Louie is unable to understand the "take it for granted" attitude of the folk at home. Each day this young soldier shops at the hospital post exchange for small Christmas gifts—writing materials, razor blades, games and small articles of food to send to the boys who remained behind when he was sent home for hospitalization.

FOUGHT WITH CHINESE.

Louie was with the "Y" forces when this American unit, consisting of medical personnel, signal corps men, ordnance teams and veterinary specialists, went into western China early in 1943 under the command of

Brig.-Gen. Frank Dorn. Their mission was to teach the Chinese how to use modern weapons and military equipment.

Louie's job was to help set up a field hospital and care for casualties from the Chinese Expeditionary Force. Side by side with Chinese, the American "Y" forces worked and fought in some of the world's most difficult terrain against Japanese positions carefully prepared for more than two years.

For 13 terrible months, during which he worked from 12 to sometimes 24 hours a day, Stephen Louie cared for shattered bodies which streamed into the hospital daily. Meager food, water which always had to be boiled, no milk, the sight of constant suffering, all added up to a rugged existence. Eventually it sent Stephen home for medical care.

Today he still finds it difficult to talk with or understand people who DAILY have more luxuries than men of the "Y" forces have seen in an entire year.

Yes, it's not hard to understand why to Pvt. Stephen Louie the Torney General Hospital is a miracle.

PALM SPRINGS, Cal., Oct. 25.

ONE of the strangest byproducts of the war is the unusual business partnership of Serna and Bernal, Inc. These long distance partners deal in conch shell, catseye and Australian and New Guinea coin costume jewelry and novelty pieces.

The U.S. half of the queer partnership, Pvt. Ray Serna, a patient at Torney General Hospital here, holds down the manufacturing end of the deal.

Somewhere in the South Pacific his buddy, Corp. Manuel Bernal, is furnishing the materials.

Serna and I are old friends. I first met him at Kirwana Island Hospital in the South Pacific. Serna had just been brought there after suffering serious hip wounds from Jap machinegun bullets in New Guinea.

"The Japs sure picked a funny day to give it to me," philosophized Serna, a native of Capitan, N. Mex. (pop. 2,000). "It happened on my 19th birthday. We were surrounded by Japs in the jungle, you see, and they clipped me just before I met you in that hospital at Kirwana."

It was Serna's touching appreciation for what his nurse had done for him at Oro Bay Hospital that helped fashion the firm of Serna and Bernal.

The nurse is Lt. Fanny Halderman, of Lawton, Okla. One day Serna overheard her express the hope somebody would send her a stainless steel wristwatch band. Bedfast and handicapped though he was, Serna showed it's mighty hard to keep an American lad down.

Calling on the technique he was perfecting at Capitan High School's manual arts class when he was drafted, Serna went to work with a knife and sandpaper. Soon Lt. Halderman's coveted band was gracing her wrist.

That got Serna started. The idea he could make other things and offer them for sale immediately hit him. He remembered the brilliantly colored shells he and Bernal had collected on the beach at Wadke Island in those nerve-wracking moments before D-hour.

Through Lt. Halderman, Serna got hold of Bernal. And with a handful of shells from South Pacific sea life and coins from Australia and New Guinea, plus his promise to keep sending same, Bernal bought his way into the Serna firm.

Serna has manufactured some amazing things since then. With a nail for a tool and some plaster of paris he ingeniously strung and mounted shells.

"Lots of fellows offered me as much as $25 for the first two bracelets I made that way," Serna revealed. "But I sent them to my grandmother and Sister Emma instead."

Until Los Angeles Communications Corps, led by Major Mabel E. Patton, presented Torney's occupational therapy ward with a complete line of jewelry work tools, Serna had been producing clever rings with a knife and hammer. His first two were heart rings beaten out of New Guinea coins. Then came in rapid succession, lockets, necklaces, earrings and pendants.

I asked if he and Bernal planned to go into the jewelry business in earnest after the war.

"I'm not quite sure, Miss Langford," he thoughtfully replied. "You know I'm a barber, too. Learned that in a C.C.C. camp in the Summer before I was drafted. I think I'll go back and finish high school first."

"You mean you didn't finish school?" I asked.

"I just missed it by six months. I was one of the first to be drafted as soon as I was 18. I kind of want to finish now, and the Government is going to help me do it, too."

And there you have a typical American, with the traditional American spirit of finishing a job once it's begun.

OAKLAND, Cal., Nov. 9.

I'D LIKE to be able to say that each and every Purple Heart cot I've visited has radiated good cheer. Truth is that oftimes even the world-famed American sense of humor can and does play hooky in a hospital.

Time hangs very heavy and long in the aisle of pain that is a military hospital ward. Entering such a humorless ward you can readily sense an atmosphere that no medicine can cure.

For medical science has never discovered a way of curing lonesomeness and the feeling of being forgotten.

Yes, conquering the ravages of their sickness and wounds is only part of the battle our hospitalized heroes must face. A very formidable foe also is the endlessness of their day in hospital beds.

Only those lying flat on their backs can know how tough it is to do nothing; can really appreciate what a sure-fire target an idle mind is for the blues and depression.

This was demonstrated very eloquently during my recent visit at Oak Knoll Naval Hospital here. The men knew in advance that I was coming. Yet patients in one ward in particular seemed surprised to see me.

As I sang, I felt a surging response from these men like I've never before received from an audience. I could hardly hit the high notes there was such a lump in my throat. Their emotions fairly rolled and broke across the ward.

A CRY IN WASHROOM.

Later a nurse explained. It seems these boys' minds had become so walled in by an oppressive lonesomeness, had grown to feel so forgotten, that they wouldn't believe the announcement I was coming to sing for them. The nurse said that seeing me had opened the door to their minds and gotten their leaden eyes to sparkle once more.

I suddenly thought what a terrible thing it would have been if I hadn't shown up. I ran to the little washroom the nurses use. There I had myself a good cry.

CORONA, Calif., Nov. 1.

ONE of the grandest groups of boys I've ever had the pleasure of singing to are the rheumatic fever patients at the U. S. Naval Hospital here.

The method of treatment for this insidious and baffling malady, even after the acute stages of the disease are past, calls for plenty of bedrest.

This enforced in activity is a bitter pill to swallow. The patient usually feels and looks well.

In most cases he's a boy, accustomed to plenty of activity all his life. You'd expect his idleness to take its toll of nervousness and irritability.

But there's no happier band of boys anywhere. You only have to talk to them a few minutes to know that the hospital staff has worked wonders in educating them to the dangers of activity not medically prescribed. For even after the symptoms of rheumatic fever have disappeared the disease can continue for several months without the victim knowing he's sick.

MARINES IN CONTROL.

When I reached Ward 443 at Norco (the Naval hospital is popularly called that), I found the Marines had the situation well in hand—same being a checker game in which Marine Pvt. Reuben C. Swenson, of Mt. Horeb, Wis., was besting Sailor Lee Polk Brown, of New York City.

The checker antagonists tossed a rare honor my way. They actually asked me to kibitz in their game. As an invited kibitzer I did a good job. We all had a lot of fun, so perhaps the result wasn't important, after all.

After the game I asked Swenson how he was faring with his rheumatic fever tussle, especially the bedrest phase.

"It's okay now, Miss Langford," Swenson related. "But it wasn't so hot at first. I thought spending so much time in bed was going to drive me nuts. A few times I felt they'd have to take away my pajama trousers to keep me from playing hooky."

HOW DOC WON HIM OVER.

"Anything happen to change your mind?" I inquired.

"Yes, there was, Miss Langford. The ward surgeon gave me quite a talking to. He explained how important it was I remain absolutely quiet. He knew I was nuts about football and warned that if I left my bed too soon I might never play football again. That did it. It was easy for me to stay in bed from there on in."

As Swenson enters the home stretch of his long convalescence, memories of his football starring days at Mt. Horeb High School flash through his mind. Thanks to the sound reasoning of the ward surgeon Swenson contentedly looks forward to the day when he'll have an opportunity to add to his store of happy gridiron memories.

Lt. Cmdr. George C. Griffith, who has devoted a lifetime to taking up the challenge of rheumatic fever, illustrated what happens when a patient is tempted from bed prematurely.

STIFF PRICE TO PAY.

"One of the lads was so homesick," he said, "that his family feigned illness and we gave him a leave, cautioning him against over-exercise. As a result the trip induced a complete recurrence with an even greater intensity and for a time it was doubtful if he could be completely reconditioned."

"That was a pretty hard price to pay for a few days at home," I said.

"Yes," Dr. Griffith agreed, adding, "if only parents and patients could understand how important it is to follow a medically prescribed regime of rest."

CORONA, Calif., Nov. 6.

NORCO, which is the popular name for the U. S. Naval Hospital here, is probably the largest rheumatic fever hospital in the world. Every member of the Navy stricken with this ailment, no matter in what theatre of the war, is either flown in or comes via transport and train to Corona as soon as it's safe for them to travel.

No man is released until his case has been observed for at least six months and he has received the OK of a Navy survey board, one member of which is Lt. Cmdr. George C. Griffith.

As I previously reported, Norco holds the amazing record of returning 85 to 90 per cent of the Navy's rheumatic fever cases back to active service. I pointed out to Dr. Griffith that a method of treatment responsible for such miraculous results should be passed on to the parents of the chief sufferers of rheumatic fever—children between the ages of five to 15 years.

EXPLAINS TREATMENT.

"The point to emphasize in treatment of this disease," Dr. Griffith stated, "is ABSOLUTE rest, plenty of sunshine and good nourishing food. Our patients are rested until breathing exercises in bed are indicated. Next come passive exercises such as flexing the hands.

"After that we start them bicycling with arms and legs while still in bed. This is followed by simple exercises which they do while standing beside their beds and ALWAYS with shoes on their feet.

"Occupational and educational therapy are introduced while the patient is still bedfast. As he progresses outdoor exercises are added. This finally culminates in six to eight hours of digging, raking, maintaining the golf course (the hospital used to be the Norconian Country Club), serving the canoes on the lake or some other indicated outdoor activity.

BOYS WORK ON FARM.

"We have a convalescent unit at Spadra where the boys can farm and be outdoors all day. And until they are graduated to this unit or have done its equivalent of work, they may not come before the survey board for release."

"What do they do for amusement besides occupational therapy?" I asked.

"You should hear our vocal hepcats in a jam session. I'll guarantee they could have beaten any of their Dad's barber shop quartets hands down."

A SLEEPY JIVER.

After seeing them, I'll bet on these fellows, too! One Marine in Ward 465 is so hep he cuts a rug even while in slumberland. While dancer Patty Thomas was beating out her taps to the strumming of a guitar, the Marine in question was hitting the hay on a top tier bed a few feet away. We all laughed as his foot started to keep time to the music. He opened one eye cautiously at first.

I told him to come on down as he was missing something. By this time he had both eyes open. One look at Miss Thomas' cute figure and he was in complete agreement with me.

"But I'm not missing it any longer," he called, carefully climbing down and joining the Marines and sailors grouped around us.

TOMORROW'S INVESTMENT.

Norco has its heart set on obtaining a printing press for its occupational therapy department. It would benefit the boys in two important ways:

Give them an interesting diversionary recreation.

Prepare the younger veterans (many of whom will be seeking their FIRST job) for a postwar vocation.

And, neighbors, anyone having a share in giving our servicemen a lift along these lines is investing in the security of the United States of tomorrow.

OAKLAND, Cal., Nov. 16.

BEFORE the war "Embraceable You" was just another song to me. A pretty tune, to be sure, but there were several melodies I liked better.

Then came the desert hospital in Kairouan, North Africa. I went into the ward where the burned men lay. Tank victims, mostly. The stench was horrible. The odor of burned flesh mingled with hospital smells.

I bent over a boy who, according to all rules, shouldn't have been alive. The boy stared, then seemingly recognized me. Silently, he started squeezing my hand. He gripped it hard and wouldn't let go.

Finally the doctor had to come and release me on the promise that I would sing to him.

Something soft was in order. "Embraceable You" is a soft song, I shall always feel a kindly Providence led me to its choice. For "Embraceable You" happened to be the favorite of that boy's sweetheart back home. Halfway through my song he began smiling—this boy who was practically dead.

SONG EASES PAIN.

Ever since then, "Embraceable You" has helped bring me closer to thousands of wounded service men. It has also helped me over the rough spots. For it's not easy to see others in pain. Sometimes you wonder how your heart can stand so much emotional squeezing.

Then you visit a hospital like Oak Knoll Naval Hospital here and you find that you can ride through an emotional storm on a song.

That is, with the help of two of my favorite marines, Pfc Dale R. Lawson, of 305 East Friendship, Newcastle, Pa. and Corp. Robert Rae, of Cleveland.

Singing for Lawson and Rae was a return engagement for me. I visited them at a base hospital on Espiritu Santo Island in the South Pacific.

It was just after Jap mortar fire had felled them during the invasion of Guam. Overseas, too, they had lain in adjoining beds.

I remembered them right away, although I hadn't learned their names in the South Pacific.

When I reached Lawson and Rae's cots at Oak Knoll, their faces showed their hunger to get something off their chests.

I greeted them like lost brothers.

"What's going on here?" I asked. "What are you boys cooking up now?"

PUT BET ON HER MEMORY.

"When we heard you were coming, Miss Langford," Lawson replied, "Bob Rae and I made ourselves a little bet with the other boys here. We've written down the song you sang to us in that overseas hospital. Our bet is that you can name it and sing it without any reminder from us."

"Well, here's where you win your bet," I laughed, starting to sing "Embraceable You."

I was facing them while I sang and it was a nice feeling seeing the grins of satisfaction and look of triumph on their faces. Throughout my song, Lawson slowly rubbed his finger.

I was about to ask him how his finger was, when I saw the gleam of metal on it. It was a wedding ring. "Embraceable You" had made him finger it caressingly as he fondly thought of his wife in far-off Newcastle, Mrs. Angela Lawson.

HOLLYWOOD, Dec. 11—WERE Sgt. Daniel Bissell of Gen. George Washington's Army alive he would be proud of the sacred regard we hold for the Military Order of the Purple Heart. He also would be proud of the deep patriotism of the Purple Heart organization, all the members of which proudly wear the decoration.

For Sgt. Bissell, member of the 2nd Connecticut Regiment, was the first recipient of the Purple Heart. I had the pleasure of meeting Dr. Frank S. Bissell, of Pasadena, and his son, Dr. Frank E. Bissell, of Hollywood, direct descendants of the first wearer of the decoration. The occasion was a recent dinner of the Military Order of the Purple Heart in Hollywood.

Even the bravest of men might well have flinched at the assignment that won Sgt. Bissell the badge of the Purple Heart under an order issued by George Washington on Aug. 7, 1782. For Bissell had to pose as a deserter form the Colonial Army, and face the brand of traitor before his family, his friends and all who loved him.

THROUGH BRITISH LINES.

But somebody was needed to penetrate the British lines and report on their strength in New York and Long Island. And the British would naturally be suspicious of any man posing as a deserter unless he were officially listed as one. So Bissell agreed to do the job.

He enrolled in Benedict Arnold's regiment. Arnold, having himself decided to betray the Revolutionary cause, didn't suspect Bissell of feeling differently. He must have read the list of deserters and smirked at the thought of all those who were ready to betray George Washington.

It took Bissell a full year to fulfill his promise to Washington. During that year he was ravaged by illness. In his delirium he talked of his true purpose in the British army. The doctor who was tending him did not betray him. Perhaps he liked Daniel Bissell too much. Perhaps he had secret sympathy for a man who would risk so much in the service of his country.

WARNED TO ESCAPE.

At any rate he warned him it was time to escape; and after some blood-curdling adventures the valiant Bissell did.

Washington wanted to reward him for his great services, for he had memorized every detail about the British army in New York which Washington needed to know. And tired and exhausted though he was when he reached American Headquarters, he had spent hours committing to paper all the secret details, maps and diagrams which would help the American cause.

Under normal circumstances Washington would have promoted Bissell to a higher rank. But Congress had taken that power out of his hands.

PURPLE HEART REWARD.

Bissell was offered a pension, but he didn't want it. And Washington, determined to reward him in some way, hit on the idea of bestowing the Purple Heart on the valiant Bissell.

Washington's order called for it to be made of purple cloth or silk edged with narrow lace or binding. It was to be worn over the left breast.

Strangely enough after Washington's death the Purple Heart decoration fell into disuse. It was not revived again until 1932, when the War Department decided this decoration should be restored in honor of Washington's memory.

The Purple Heart has a proud history, and every man who earns one today is descended in spirit from Daniel Bissell, who gave his health and risked his life to help free his country.

VAN NUYS, Calif., Feb. 29—When I first met 26-year-old Clifford Roland he was lying on a cot at the North Sector General Hospital in Hawaii. I had stopped off there on my South Pacific tour.

He was a typical overseas GI then—lonesome for his wife, Edith; anxious to get back to his job of developing film for the Monarch Photo Co., of Los Angeles. His world was not very bright. Enthusiasm was only a word in a dictionary as far as he was concerned.

I saw him again today and it was hard to believe he's the same person. Enthusiasm fairly oozed from his bed. All because a belated high school diploma has given him a new lease on life.

NEAR HOME.

Clifford is convalescing at the Army's big Birmingham General Hospital in the sun-soaked San Fernando Valley, 10 miles from Hollywood. He's close to home again—Los Angeles is his home. He's near his wife and old friends. This, of course, has given him a lot of solid satisfaction. But it hasn't been as exciting as getting that diploma.

"When I was overseas, Frances," Clifford explained, "I used to give a lot of thought to my future. My one great worry was knowing I didn't have a high school education. Today the good jobs require it."

I asked him why he hadn't completed his education.

"When I was 17," he replied, "I had a series of illnesses. I was in and out of school because of it. Finally, I got so far behind that I just gave up. Then, when I was 21, I went back and tried to finish, but again I landed behind the eight-ball. So I gave up trying. When I was 23 I got married. Edith's a swell girl. She had graduated from Venice High School and I felt I owed it to her to at least match her schooling. But the odds seemed to be against me."

IN GILBERT'S INVASION.

Clifford was overseas 11 months, was in the invasion of the Gilbert Islands and saw plenty of combat hell on earth. When the medics decided to send him back to this country, he made mental plans for the day when he'd take his old job in the photo lab.

He hadn't been a patient at Birmingham Hospital more than 24 hours when the reconditioning officials there asked him what he'd most like to do after the war.

"I'd like to finish high school," he told them wistfully, not dreaming for a moment that it was possible.

The next day he was enrolled in the hospital's high school course. He gave it all the time permitted by hospital regulations. He worked hard, almost feverishly, to make the grade.

And he made it! This week his wife, Edith, stood beside him at graduating exercises held at the hospital. He was given a diploma and the most happiness he can ever remember.

"You know what I'm planning on now?" he asked me. "I'm not going to be satisfied with my old job of developing prints. I'm going to try to work up in that company and be one of the managers someday. Maybe even an executive!"

Hollywood, May 13 [1950]—After talking with hundreds of hospitalized ex-GIs, you can't help learning a few things about them.

One of the things I've learned that they haven't forgotten: they cried to God for help when the going was tough.

I don't mean that they've sprouted wings. But I do mean they have acquired a deeper understanding of religion.

Many of my friends along Purple Heart Row will tell you, without being asked, that prayer works.

They will tell you that all the money in the world couldn't have done for them what prayer did. That without prayer they couldn't have taken the manifold tortures their bodies and mind have withstood on the battlefield and in the hospital wards.

"There wasn't a man in my outfit who didn't feel close to God," an ex-paratrooper told me recently. "I'll never forget how we prayed together before our jumps. It was like talking to God on his own private line."

This ex-warrior strongly feels he wouldn't be here if he hadn't had those talks with God.

"I was lying wounded in a pool of my own blood," he related. "I was getting weaker and weaker from the loss of blood. I felt God had to take care of me because I couldn't take care of myself. So I prayed."

He lost consciousness then. When he woke up, a soldier's hand was holding his.

"Only God could have directed that hand," he said. "Because it didn't belong to one of our men. It belonged to a young Nazi. He was there to help me, not hurt me."

APPENDIX 3

Frances Langford Radio Credits

The Fleischmann Hour (**February 12, 1931**) NBC, Standard Brands, Inc.
Series regular is Rudy Vallee. Frances Langford is the guest vocalist, supposedly a Vallee discovery when he was in Florida. Reportedly, this was her first radio appearance behind the mike.

The Fleischmann Hour (**June 25, 1931**) NBC, Standard Brands, Inc.
Series regular is Rudy Vallee. Frances Langford is the guest vocalist on this program.

Melody Kaleidoscope (**July 20, 1931, to August 17, 1931**) Mutual
Emil Velazco plays the organ while Frances Langford supplies the vocals.

Assorted Music Filler (August 5, 1931, through 1934) Mutual
Frances Langford was hired as a singer on WOR, the flagship station of the Mutual Broadcasting System. She sang in ten-, fifteen- and thirty-minute increments on various days and time slots.

Music With Frances Langford (**November 6, 1931, to February 5, 1932**) Mutual
Friday evening program starring Frances Langford. Beginning with the broadcast of January 8, Jack Arthur was added to the weekly program.

Knight's Orchestra (**June 8, 1932, to July 20, 1932**) Mutual
   Frances Langford and Gene Charles were series regulars providing vocals with Norvell Knight and his Orchestra on this short-lived Wednesday evening musical offering.

NBC Solo Performances (circa March 1933 to December 1933) NBC
   Beginning in March 1933, Langford was no longer under exclusive contract with Mutual and began filling in assorted time slots at the NBC studios, including late-night performances with Jesse Crawford at the organ.

Lum and Abner (**June or July 1933**) NBC, Ford Motors
   Frances Langford sings "Young and Healthy" during a Friday night sociable at the Pine Ridge Schoolhouse.

The Spartan Hour (**January 7, 1934, to February 11, 1934**) NBC, Spartan Radio Company
   A half-hour musical offering on Sunday afternoons with Richard Himber and his Orchestra supplying the music and Frances Langford the vocals.

The Colgate House Party (**March 3, 1934, to June 2, 1934**) NBC, Colgate
   Joe Cook's weekly comedy-variety program featured the music of Donald Voorhees and his Orchestra, with vocals by Frances Langford.

The Ed Sullivan Show (**March 21, 1934**) NBC
   Series regular Ed Sullivan plays host to a broadcast of talent. Vincent Lopez and his Orchestra provide the music. Frances Langford was the guest on this program, supplying vocals.

The Colgate House Party (**June 11, 1934, to December 10, 1934**) NBC, Colgate
   Joe Cook's weekly comedy-variety program featured the music of Donald Voorhees and his Orchestra, with vocals by Frances Langford. Cook left the program after the broadcast of November 12 and Langford was replaced by Martha Mears, contralto, beginning December 17, 1934. (Langford was unable to attend the November 12 broadcast.) The program continued with Mears, Conrad Thibault, and the Goodman Orchestra through January 21, 1935.

Hollywood Hotel **(October 5, 1934, to December 2, 1938)** CBS, The Campbell Soup Company

Hosted by Hollywood gossip columnist Louella Parsons, this weekly program offered dramatic sketches with Hollywood celebrities and a musical number by series regular Frances Langford. The only exceptions are Lois Ravel from October 23 to November 6, 1936, Shirley Ross from April 16 to May 7, 1937, and Loretta Lee from November 19 to December 3, 1937.

The Lucky Strike Hit Parade **(a.k.a. *The Big Broadcast*, September 14, 1935)** NBC

A special hour-long broadcast from Los Angeles with appearances from radio, stage and screen personalities. Frances Langford was among the celebrity guests.

MGM Syndicated Air Trailers (circa 1935 - 1938) Syndicated

Produced at MGM Studios in California, these fifteen-minute commercial promos for up-coming motion pictures were specifically recorded for radio broadcast. Also contains audio tracks from the movies. Extant recordings include *Music is Magic* (1935), *Broadway Melody of 1936* (1935), *Born to Dance* (1936), *Palm Springs* (1936), and *Collegiate* (1936).

The George Burns and Gracie Allen Show **(circa 1936)** CBS, Campbell Soup Company

George Burns and Gracie Allen were the weekly regulars. For reasons unknown the stars were unable to attend one broadcast in 1936 so Dick Powell and Frances Langford, series regulars on Campbell's *Hollywood Hotel*, assumed the spotlight and performed a Burns and Allen routine. Langford sang "You Turned the Tables on Me."

Al Lyons Orchestra **(circa 1936, Program #2656)** Community Chest Syndication

Recorded from the Cocoanut Grove in Hollywood. Frances Langford provides the vocals.

The Frank Morgan Show **(May 26, 1937, to September 1, 1937)** WHN in New York City

Fifteen-minute variety program with series regular Frank Morgan, Freddie Rich and his Orchestra and Frances Langford supplying the vocals.

National Mobilization for Human Needs (**circa 1938**) Community Chest Fund Appeal

A fifteen-minute fundraiser recorded in November 1938 and syndicated during the holiday in an effort to convince radio listeners to donate money to their local Community Chest. Ralph Bellamy is interviewed about his latest movie, *Trade Winds*. Frances Langford sings "I Feel A Song Coming On."

The Texaco Star Theatre (**January 4, 1939, to June 28, 1939**) CBS, Texaco Oil

Weekly hour-long program with a half-hour of music and a half-hour of drama. Frances Langford and Kenny Baker supplied vocals for this broadcast. The program premiered October 5, 1938, and Langford replaced series regular Jane Froman beginning January 4, 1939. For the broadcast of May 31, 1939, Langford joined Jon Hall in a drama titled "The Beach Boy."

Kraft Music Hall (**March 9, 1939**) NBC, Kraft Foods

Series regulars are Bing Crosby and John Scott Trotter and his Orchestra. Frances Langford is a guest singer for this broadcast.

The Royal Gelatin Hour (**May 18, 1939**) NBC, Standard Brands, Inc.

Rudy Vallee was the series regular, celebrating his 500th radio broadcast on this evening with celebrity guests Lee de Forest, Cliff Arquette, Frances Langford, Edgar Bergen and Charlie McCarthy.

The Texaco Star Theatre (**September 13, 1939, to June 26, 1940**) CBS, Texaco Oil

Hour-long weekly variety program featuring music, drama and comedy. Kenny Baker, Irene Ryan and Frances Langford are the series regulars. The musical half of the program originated from Hollywood, the dramatic half from New York City.

Rudy Vallee Alumni Reunion (**March 1, 1940**) NBC, National Dairy Products Corporation

This half-hour special was broadcast from a testimonial dinner in Rudy Vallee's honor, a reunion of friends with comedy routines and music. Eddie Cantor was the toastmaster. Celebrity guests included George Burns and Gracie Allen, Arthur Q. Bryan, Bob Burns and Frances Langford.

Chicago Variety **(October 10, 1940)** Mutual
Frances Langford is the guest for this broadcast, performing a couple of musical numbers.

Musical Americana **(October 31, 1940)** NBC
Frances Langford is a guest singer with Raymond Paige and his Orchestra.

Frances Langford and the News (November 19 and 26, 1940) WHN in New York City
Following a brief five minutes of news, Frances Langford filled in as guest singer for the remaining ten minutes over WHN in New York City.

Greek War Relief Fund **(February 25, 1941)** NBC
The Greek War Relief is mentioned only in passing by Bob Hope during the program. The unstated purpose of the program was the ongoing conflict of BMI and ASCAP with the broadcast industry. Numerous singers and songwriters lent their talents in defiance of the present-day issue: Frances Langford, Judy Garland, Jack Benny, Harry Warren, Mary Martin, Harry Ruby, Hoagy Carmichael, Jerome Kern, Dinah Shore, Margaret Whiting, Cole Porter and many others. Only thirty minutes of this 2 ½ hour event was broadcast over NBC in New York City. The program was never heard over the West Coast.

The Gulf Screen Guild Theatre **(March 9, 1941)** CBS, Gulf Oil Company
Weekly anthology featuring Hollywood actors reprising their film roles for radio adaptations of popular movies. In this broadcast, Fibber McGee and Molly venture West to make a movie, promoting their upcoming picture. Celebrity guests include Edward Arnold, Joan Bennett, Gary Cooper and Frances Langford.

The Pepsodent Show **(May 6, 1941)** NBC, Lever Brothers
Bob Hope's first program to originate from a naval base. This was broadcast from Muroc, California. Jerry Colonna and Barbara Jo Allen are series regulars. Frances Langford is the guest.

Southern Cruise **(July 4, 1941, to August 15, 1941)** CBS
A musical company visited Latin-American ports of call on an ocean liner. Lead vocalists each week were Dick Powell and Frances Langford

with the musical assistance of Lud Gluskin and his Orchestra. The name of the program changed to *American Cruise* for the final three broadcasts of the series. *American Cruise* continued for a number of weeks on a different day of the week, with Gluskin and his Orchestra taking the helm and Gertrude Niesen as the weekly regular.

Stars Over Hollywood (September 13, 1941) CBS, Dari-Rich
Weekly Saturday afternoon anthology. Frances Langford played the starring role in "Contract With No Options."

The Pepsodent Show (September 23, 1941, to June 16, 1942) NBC, Lever Brothers
Series regular is Bob Hope. Jerry Colonna provides comedy backup and Frances Langford is now a regular providing at least one song in each show. A number of the radio broadcasts this season originated from other parts of the country, including San Francisco and Cleveland.

Your Hit Parade (March 14, 1942) CBS, R.J. Reynolds Tobacco Company
Series regulars Barry Wood and Joan Edwards are assisted by guest Frances Langford in singing the top songs of the week.

Command Performance (Program #10, recorded April 23, 1942) AFRS
Wartime broadcast recorded in a studio with Hollywood performers lending their talents to entertain troops stationed overseas. *Command Performance* was never broadcast in the United States. Each episode was recorded on a platter and shipped across the ocean for the benefit of U.S. soldiers stationed overseas. Celebrity guests include George Burns and Gracie Allen, Maxie Rosenbloom and Frances Langford.

Command Performance (Program #23, recorded July 21, 1942) AFRS
Celebrity guests include the cast of *The Great Gildersleeve* with Harold Peary, Lillian Randolph and Walter Tetley. Dick Powell and Frances Langford both sing a song, solo.

Mail Call (Program #1, recorded August 11, 1942) AFRS
Recorded for the benefit of U.S. troops stationed overseas, not broadcast in the U.S. Bob Hope does a simulated Air Corps training field broadcast with Jerry Colonna and Frances Langford.

Command Performance (**Program #37, recorded October 21, 1942**) AFRS
Frances Langford is the emcee for this broadcast. Celebrity guests include Bob Burns, Helen O'Connell, and Jimmy Dorsey and his Orchestra.

The Pepsodent Show (**September 22, 1942, to June 15, 1943**) NBC, Lever Brothers
Series regular is Bob Hope. Jerry Colonna and Barbara Jo Allen are series regulars, along with Frances Langford who sings at least one song per broadcast. By this time Hope had convinced the sponsors to take the program on the road and almost every episode originated from a naval base stationed across the country.

Treasury Star Parade (**Program #341, circa 1943-44**)
Produced by the Treasury Department for syndication. Frances Langford provides the vocals, including "People Will Say We're In Love."

Command Performance (**Program #53, recorded February 20, 1943**) AFRS
Frances Langford starts the show by singing "Saving Myself For Bill." Allan Jones performs his signature "Donkey Serenade." Kay Kyser and his Orchestra supply music along with Jimmy Wakely and the Rough Riders.

Camel Comedy Caravan (**June 4, 1943**) CBS, R.J. Reynolds Tobacco Company
Connie Boswell, Lanny Ross and Herb Shriner made way for weekly guest stars during the summer months. For this broadcast Bob Hope, Jerry Colonna and Frances Langford provided the evening entertainment.

Frances Langford Records (**June 19, 1943, to July 10, 1943**) WMCA in New York City
Fifteen-minute musical program with performances by Frances Langford.

War Telescope (**July 3, 1943**) NBC
Weekly overseas news program with Morgan Beatty in London interviewing Bob Hope and Frances Langford on this particular broadcast. Hope explains the procedure for performing 3 or 4 shows a day for troops stationed overseas.

The Pepsodent Show (**September 21, 1943, to May 30, 1944**) NBC, Lever Brothers
Series regular is Bob Hope. Jerry Colonna and Barbara Jo Allen are series regulars, along with Frances Langford who sings at least one song per broadcast.

Command Performance (**Program #86, recorded September 25, 1943**) AFRS
Celebrity guests include Bob Hope, Bing Crosby, Tony Romano and Frances Langford.

Soldiers in Greasepaint (**November 25, 1943**) NBC, sustaining
A special 45-minute Thanksgiving broadcast during the noon hour saluting the U.S.O. Celebrity guests include Al Jolson, Bob Hope, Andy Devine, Carole Landis, Mitzi Mayfair, Merle Oberon, Martha Raye, Kay Francis, John Garfield, Judith Anderson, Jack Benny, Fredric March, Anna Lee, Fay McKenzie, Jinx Falkenburg and Frances Langford.

Second Annual Tribute to the Armed Forces (**November 25, 1943**) CBS, Elgin Watches
Two-hour Thanksgiving special reminding radio listeners of soldiers who have to serve turkey to each other instead of with their families. Frank Lovejoy performs a battlefield drama. Gracie Allen tells George Burns that she invited a few servicemen over for Thanksgiving dinner. Edgar Bergen tells Charlie McCarthy about the story of Pocahontas. José Iturbi, Danny O'Neill, The Pied Pipers and Frances Langford perform musical numbers.

Command Performance (**Program #94, recorded November 27, 1943**) AFRS
Edgar Bergen tells Charlie McCarthy the story of *Oliver Twist*. Bob Wills and The Texas Playboys perform country music, including "New San Antonio Rose." Virginia O'Brien deadpans "In a Little Spanish Town." Frances Langford lends her vocal talents.

Command Performance (**Program #96, recorded December 11, 1943**) AFRS
This program is dedicated to the AEF North African Network, celebrating their first anniversary on the air. Martha Raye sings "Mr.

Paganini." The cast of *Four Jills in a Jeep* (including Kay Francis and Mitzi Mayfair) perform a sketch. Frances Langford sings a song. Bob Hope is emcee.

Command Performance (recorded November 6, 1943) AFRS

Special 90-minute Christmas broadcast with Bob Hope as the emcee. Celebrity guests include Spike Jones and his City Slickers, Kay Kyser and his Orchestra, Nelson Eddy, Fred Allen, Dinah Shore, Ed Gardner, Ginny Simms and Frances Langford.

Special Christmas Show (December 25, 1943) NBC

Hour-long special for the holidays with Robert Armbruster and his Orchestra, Lewis Stone and Frances Langford.

To the Rear March (Program #79, circa 1944) AFRS

Features a rebroadcast of *The Pepsodent Show* from December 28, 1943, with Bob Hope, Jerry Colonna, Barbara Jo Allen and Frances Langford.

Command Performance (Program #101, recorded January 15, 1944) AFRS

Frances Langford doubles as host and guest singer. Langford sings the first song, "Shoo Shoo, Baby." Spike Jones and his City Slickers, Virginia O'Brien and Jimmy Wakely also provide musical entertainment.

March of Dimes Special (January 29, 1944) All networks, The March of Dimes

One-hour special saluting President Roosevelt's birthday with stars of radio, stage and screen. Program originates from the Waldorf Astoria in New York City. Celebrity guests include Bob Hope, Georgia Gibbs, Jerry Colonna, Mary Pickford, Lily Pons, Jimmy Durante, Frank Sinatra, Eddie Cantor, Dinah Shore and Frances Langford.

The Cavalcade of America (February 14, 1944) NBC, E.I. du Pont de Nemours and Company

In recognition of Valentine's Day, and troops stationed overseas missing their loved ones, DuPont temporarily shelved their weekly dramatic offering to present Frances Langford's recollection of her summer 1943 U.S.O. tour in Alaska, England and North Africa. Langford also sings "Please Don't Cry."

Command Performance (**Program #107, recorded February 19, 1944**) AFRS

Loretta Young is the emcee. Three female singers provide numerous melodies to remind the troops stationed overseas what they were fighting for. Guests include Frances Langford, Ginny Simms and Connie Boswell.

Command Performance (**Program #114, recorded April 8, 1944**) AFRS

Jerry Colonna is the emcee. Celebrity guests include Connie Haines, Jo Stafford and Frances Langford.

Mail Call (**Program #90, recorded May 10, 1944**) AFRS

This broadcast is a tribute to the state of Florida. Judy Canova sings "Shortnin' Bread." Jerry Colonna provides a lecture about Florida. Frances Langford is the emcee.

Command Performance (**Program #119, recorded May 13, 1944**) AFRS

Jerry Colonna is the emcee. Celebrity guests include Frances Langford, Lena Horne, Helen Forrest and Dinah Shore.

Command Performance (**Program #123, recorded June 3, 1944**) AFRS

Shirley Ross sings "Thanks for the Memory." Connie Haines is the emcee. Celebrity guests include Bob Hope, Jerry Colonna, Frances Langford, Lotte Lehmann and Lena Horne.

Your All-Time Hit Parade (**July 2, 1944**) NBC, R.J. Reynolds Tobacco Company

Tommy Dorsey and his Orchestra supplies music. Frances Langford is the guest singer.

The Pepsodent Show (**September 12, 1944, to June 5, 1945**) NBC, Lever Brothers

Series regular is Bob Hope. Jerry Colonna and Barbara Jo Allen are series regulars, along with Frances Langford who sings at least one song per broadcast.

Command Performance (**Program #138, recorded September 13, 1944**) AFRS

Bob Hope is the emcee. Celebrity guests include Johnny Mercer, Jerry Colonna, Beatrice Kay, Frances Langford, Gloria DeHaven, June

Allyson and Jane Russell.

Mail Call (**Program #113, recorded October 11, 1944**) AFRS
This broadcast is a salute to the China-Burma-India Theatre. Celebrity guests include Frances Langford, Sterling Holloway, William Demarest, Larry Adler and Jerry Colonna.

The Cavalcade of America (**October 16, 1944**) NBC, E.I. du Pont de Nemours and Company
Frances Langford, Bob Hope and Jerry Colonna star in a "Report from the Pacific," a dramatized tour of the front lines with Hope and his crew entertaining troops stationed overseas during the summer 1944 USO tour. Tony Romano supplies guitar music.

Special Thanksgiving Day Program (**Nov. 23, 1944**) CBS, Elgin Watches
Two-hour broadcast with celebrity guests Jimmy Durante, Garry Moore, Elsie Janis, Spike Jones and his City Slickers, Edgar Bergen and Charlie McCarthy, Ed Gardner and Frances Langford.

Which is Which? (**December 6, 1944**) CBS, Lorillard Tobacco Company
A game show in which the contestants have to guess whether they are listening to a Hollywood celebrity or a voice impersonator. Celebrity guests include Sydney Greenstreet, Eric Blore, Richard Nelson and Frances Langford.

Command Performance (**recorded October 1944**) AFRS
Special two-hour Christmas 1944 broadcast with Bob Hope as the emcee. Celebrity guests include Jerry Colonna, Spencer Tracy, Judy Garland, W.C. Fields, Danny Kaye, Kay Kyser, Fred Allen, Jack Benny, Dinah Shore, Johnny Mercer, Lee J. Cobb, Ginny Simms, Jimmy Durante and Frances Langford.

Music for Millions (**Program #12, circa 1945**) Treasury Department syndication
Sponsored by the Victory Loan Drive this short-lived syndicated program aired on various stations across the country through 1945 to help boost sales of war bonds. Frances Langford is the celebrity guest for this episode, assisted by Victor Young and his Orchestra, performing a brand-new song, "Now's the Time to Buy a Bond."

The Lux Radio Theatre (**January 8, 1945**) CBS, Lever Brothers
This program offered an adaptation of a popular Hollywood movie with the original actors, whenever possible, reprising their film roles. For this broadcast, the producers of *Lux* departed from the usual format to present Bob Hope, Jerry Colonna and Frances Langford in the lead of "I Never Left Home," adapted from Hope's book of the same name. This hour-long presentation dramatized Hope's trip overseas to entertain the troops during wartime.

Stage Door Canteen (**January 19, 1945**) CBS, Corn Products
Musical variety program with Raymond Paige and his Orchestra. Guest stars for this broadcast include Jane Withers, Lee Bowman and Frances Langford.

Mail Call (**Program #133, recorded February 21, 1945**) AFRS
Jack Carson is the emcee. Celebrity guests include Herbert Marshall, Jerry Colonna and Franklin Pangborn. Frances Langford sings "There Goes That Song Again."

The Radio Hall of Fame (**February 25, 1945**) Blue Network, Philco Radio Corp.
This program originates from the Earl Carroll Theatre Restaurant in Hollywood. Frances Langford is the emcee. Celebrity guests include Nigel Bruce, Alan Reed, Johnny Mercer and Ed Gardner.

Command Performance (**Program #165, recorded March 8, 1945**) AFRS
Frank Sinatra is the emcee. Celebrity guests include Bing Crosby, Peggy Ann Garner, Roddy McDowall, Margaret O'Brien, Elizabeth Taylor, Gary Crosby and Frances Langford.

The V-E Day Special (**Program #5, May 8, 1945**) AFRS
Celebrity guests include Ginny Simms, Herbert Marshall, Charles Boyer, Johnny Mercer, Judy Garland, Loretta Young, Bing Crosby, Bob Hope and Frances Langford.

The Seventh War Loan Drive (**May 13, 1945**) NBC
Bob Hope is emcee. This program originates from the Uline Arena in Washington, D.C. Celebrity guests include Barbara Jo Allen, Jerry Colonna and Frances Langford.

The Chase and Sanborn Program (**June 5, 1945, to August 26, 1945**)
NBC, Standard Brands

Summer replacement for Edgar Bergen and Charlie McCarthy with the same sponsor unwilling to relinquish the time slot. Musical program featured series regulars Spike Jones and his City Slickers, Tony Romano and Frances Langford. Every week the program originated from an army hospital, naval hospital or training station.

Armed Forces V-J Program (**September 2, 1945**) AFRS

Celebrity guests include Dinah Shore, Bob Hope, Bing Crosby, Frank Sinatra, Orson Welles, Harry Truman and Frances Langford.

The Pepsodent Show (**September 11, 1945, to June 11, 1946**) NBC, Lever Brothers

Series regular is Bob Hope. Jerry Colonna and Skinnay Ennis are series regulars, along with Frances Langford who sings at least one song per broadcast.

The Victory Chest Program (**September 29, 1945**) All Networks, Victory Chest Fund

This two-and-a-half-hour special originated from the Hollywood Bowl in honor of the 25th anniversary of broadcasting. Only thirty minutes of the show aired over Mutual. Other networks chose to broadcast selected time periods during the evening in different areas of the country. Celebrity guests include Jack Carson, Edward G. Robinson, Gene Autry, Frank Sinatra, Eddie Cantor, Dinah Shore, Kay Kyser, Lionel Barrymore, Bob Hope and Frances Langford.

Request Performance (**October 7, 1945**) CBS, The Campbell Soup Company

Frances Langford is guest hostess, introducing the premiere of this weekly variety program as "the first post-war radio program." Ronald Colman and Langford sing a duet, "Come Down to New Orleans."

Songs by Sinatra (**October 10, 1945**) CBS, Lorillard Tobacco Company

Series regular Frank Sinatra performs with guests Ginny Simms and Frances Langford.

Command Performance (**Program #199, recorded November 8, 1945**) AFRS
Frances Langford is the guest emcee and starts the show off with a rendition of "It's Been a Long, Long Time." Celebrity guests included Bob Crosby, Harold Peary and Walter Tetley.

Command Performance (**recorded September 13, 1945**) AFRS
Special two-hour Christmas broadcast with Bob Hope as the emcee. Celebrity guests include Herbert Marshall, Ed Gardner, Judy Garland, Johnny Mercer, Bing Crosby, Dinah Shore, Mel Blanc, Frank Sinatra, Kay Kyser, Jerry Colonna, Jimmy Durante, Cass Daley and Frances Langford.

Here's to Veterans (**Program #33, circa 1946**)
Produced by the Veterans Administration for syndication. Features Danny Thomas for a brief comedic scene, and Don Ameche and Frances Langford reprising their roles as The Bickersons.

Request Performance (**February 17, 1946**) CBS, The Campbell Soup Company
Eddie Cantor is the guest emcee. Celebrity guests include Art Linkletter, David Niven and Frances Langford.

American Cancer Society Program (**April 19, 1946**) Mutual, The American Cancer Society
Bob Hope is the emcee. Celebrity guests include Tony Martin and Frances Langford.

Maxwell House Coffee Time (**May 2, 1946**) NBC, General Foods
This is an extended one-hour special replacing the weekly *Birdseye Open House* program. Frances Langford replaces the series regular, Dinah Shore, who is suffering from laryngitis. Celebrity guests include George Burns and Gracie Allen, Charles Boyer and Mel Blanc.

Command Performance (**recorded May 29, 1946**) AFRS
This is the 90-minute fourth-anniversary program. Bob Hope is the emcee, hosting various audio clips from prior *Command Performance* broadcasts. Celebrity guests include Fred MacMurray, Janet Blair, Donald Crisp, Mel Blanc, Edgar Bergen, Kay Kyser, Jerry Colonna, Linda Darnell and Frances Langford.

The Drene Show (**December 15, 1946, to June 1, 1947**) NBC, Drene

The Drene Show premiered on the evening of September 8, 1946, with Don Ameche assisting Pinky Lee in the comedy sketches. Frances Langford replaced Lee beginning with the broadcast of December 15. She and Ameche play the roles of John and Blanche Bickerson.

The Purple Heart Theatre (**December 25, 1946**) AFRS

Frances Langford introduces Christmas records starting with "Santa Claus is Coming to Town." This thirty-minute special was recorded and broadcast for the benefit of U.S. troops stationed overseas. Langford provides a moving, inspirational Christmas message to wounded G.I.'s.

Mail Call (**Program #233, recorded circa 1947**) AFRS

Cathy Downs is the guest emcee. Celebrity guests include Dick Haymes, Jerry Colonna, Jimmy Durante and Frances Langford.

WOR 25th Anniversary Broadcast (**February 22, 1947**) Mutual, sustaining

This two-hour special acknowledges the 25th anniversary of radio station WOR, in New York City, the flagship station for the Mutual Broadcasting System. Celebrity guests include Dennis Day, Billie Burke, Bob Burns, Basil Rathbone, Dana Andrews, Babe Ruth, Guy Lombardo, Vic Damone, Tommy Dorsey, Ella Fitzgerald and Frances Langford.

Lum and Abner (**April 24, 1947**) ABC, Alka-Seltzer

Lum and Abner are celebrating their 16th year in radio with an all-star extravaganza. Celebrity guests include Jim and Marian Jordan, Kay Kyser, Don Wilson, Herbert Marshall, Phil Harris, Edna Best, Gail Patrick, Jack Bailey and Frances Langford.

Maxwell House Coffee Time (**May 29, 1947**) NBC, General Foods

Series regulars George Burns and Gracie Allen are trying to decide where to spend their vacation. Frances Langford is guest on the program to promote her weekly summer series airing in the same slot next week. Langford sings "You Belong to My Heart."

Maxwell House Coffee Time (June 5, 1947, to August 28, 1947) NBC, General Foods

Short-run summer series featuring musical numbers by series regulars Eloise Dragon, Frances Langford and the Dick Davis Chorus. Carmen Dragon conducts the orchestra.

Here's to Veterans (Program #56, recorded July 16, 1947) Veterans Administration syndication

Frances Langford is the guest celebrity in what can be considered an abbreviated version of the *Maxwell House Coffee Time*. Carmen Dragon conducts the orchestra.

The Old Gold Show (a.k.a. *The Don Ameche Show*) (September 24, 1947, to December 24, 1947) CBS, Lorillard Tobacco Company

Don Ameche and Frances Langford play the roles of John and Blanche Bickerson in this weekly comedy sketch. Marvin Miller is the announcer.

The Bickersons (recorded December 13, 1947)

An audition recording for a proposed weekly situation comedy with Don Ameche and Frances Langford playing the roles of John and Blanche Bickerson. The audition was never broadcast. Marvin Miller is the announcer.

The Pepsodent Show (December 23, 1947) NBC, Lever Brothers

Series regulars Bob Hope, Jerry Colonna and Barbara Jo Allen are treated to a reunion with Frances Langford for their Christmas offering of the year.

The Old Gold Show (a.k.a. *The Don Ameche Show*) (January 2, 1948, to June 28, 1948) CBS, Lorillard Tobacco Company

Don Ameche and Frances Langford play the roles of John and Blanche Bickerson in this weekly comedy sketch. Marvin Miller is the announcer.

U.S.O. Farewell Program (January 11, 1948) NBC, sustaining

A celebration of the conclusion of U.S.O. camp shows. Celebrity guests include Bob Hope, Jack Benny, Marlene Dietrich, Dinah Shore, Danny Thomas, Audie Murphy, Eddie Cantor, Douglas Fairbanks and Frances Langford.

Motion Picture Academy Awards (**March 20, 1948**) NBC
Celebrities Dennis Day, Dinah Shore, Jean Hersholt, Gordon MacRae and Frances Langford lent their talents for the radio coverage of the ceremony which recognizes the best movies of 1947.

Leo Forbstein Memorial Special (**April 25, 1948**) KFWB, Los Angeles
A special memorial broadcast regionally in Los Angeles for Leo Forbstein, an American composer of music for numerous motion pictures, including some of the most popular Warner Bros. releases, who passed away a month prior. Celebrities included Jack L. Warner, Al Jolson, Eddie Cantor, Dinah Shore, Danny Kaye, Doris Day, Dennis Morgan and Frances Langford.

Ted Dale and his Orchestra (**May 24, 1948**) NBC
Celebrity guest for this broadcast is Frances Langford.

Mail Call (**Program #300, recorded May 25, 1948**) AFRS
Chili Williams is the emcee for a collection of audio clips from prior *Mail Call* broadcasts. Celebrity guests include Garry Moore, Carole Landis and Frances Langford.

The Joan Davis Show (**June 19, 1948**) CBS, sustained
Series regular Joan Davis provides comedy and music with celebrity guests Jon Hall and Frances Langford.

Tex and Jinx Show (**a.k.a. *Hi Jix*, July 21, 1948**) NBC
Series regulars Tex McCrary and Jinx Falkenburg interview celebrity guests Frances Langford and Audie Murphy.

Roll Call (**July 22, 1948**) NBC
Series regular Burgess Meredith hosts celebrity guests Morton Downey, Paul Winchell and Frances Langford.

Symphonies Under the Stars (**August 5, 1948**) AFRS
Part of an on-going series produced by the AFRS, originating from the Hollywood Bowl. Celebrity guests include Red Skelton, Danny Kaye, Ed Gardner, Virginia O'Brien, Irving Berlin, Gene Autry, Edgar Bergen, Frankie Laine, Jimmy Durante, Frank Sinatra and Frances Langford.

Guest Star (Program #84, recorded October 31, 1948)
Produced by the Treasury Department for syndication, this episode aired at various days and times across the country. Frances Langford was the guest for this episode, providing vocals.

The Railroad Hour **(November 22, 1948)** ABC, The Association of American Railroads
A musical adaptation of *Hit the Deck* with Frances Langford and Gordon MacRae in the leads.

Thanksgiving Day Special **(November 25, 1948)** NBC, Elgin Watches
This was the seventh-annual Thanksgiving Day special sponsored by Elgin Watches. Dean Martin is introduced as a promising "newcomer" and a "star of tomorrow." Celebrity guests for this two-hour extravaganza included Garry Moore, Jimmy Durante, Mario Lanza, Barbara Jo Allen, Jerry Lewis, Red Skelton, Jack Benny, Don Ameche and Frances Langford.

Let's Keep Going: USO Camp Shows **(February 4, 1949)** NBC
Half-hour special with celebrity guests Madeleine Carroll, Charles Boyer, Garry Moore, Robert Merrill and Frances Langford.

The Martin and Lewis Show **(July 26, 1949)** NBC, sustaining
Series regulars are Dean Martin and Jerry Lewis. Dean wants to make a record with guest Frances Langford, which makes Jerry suspect they are breaking up their partnership.

Red Feather Preview **(October 28, 1949)** Mutual
Radio special with celebrity guests Garry Moore, Bob Hope, Jimmy Durante and Frances Langford.

Duffy's Tavern **(February 2, 1950)** NBC
Stars Ed Gardner as Archie the barkeep in this situation comedy. Celebrity guests include Jon Hall and Frances Langford.

Music by Faith **(Program #68, recorded September 10, 1950)** AFRS
Percy Faith and his Orchestra supplied the music, Frances Langford the vocals.

Stars on Parade (**Program #541, February 16, 1951**)
Produced by the Army and Army Air Force for syndication, with the intent of recruiting. Frances Langford is the guest singer.

This is New York (**February 24, 1951**) CBS
Hosted by Bill Leonard. Celebrity guest is Frances Langford.

The Bickersons (**June 5, 1951, to August 28, 1951**) CBS, Philip Morris Cigarettes
A short-lived summer series with Lew Parker and Frances Langford as John and Blanche Bickerson. Tony Romano and his Orchestra provide the music.

Mail Call (**Program #151, recorded June 27, 1951**) AFRS
While Ed Gardner is on a U.S.O. tour, Frances Langford visits Eddie the waiter and Clifton Finnegan down at Duffy's Tavern. Langford is also the emcee.

A Parade of Music (**January 28, 1954**) NBC
A salute to the March of Dimes with celebrities Lanny Ross, Robert Merrill and Frances Langford.

Recollections at Thirty (**July 4, 1956**) NBC, sustaining
A collection of vintage radio recordings, including Clark and McCullough making their first radio appearance, Al Jolson on *Shell Chateau* and a brief clip of Frances Langford sharing the microphone with Lum and Abner.

Recollections at Thirty (**March 20, 1957**) NBC, sustaining
A collection of vintage radio recordings from 1933, including President Roosevelt's inaugural speech, Ed Wynn, Graham McNamee, "The Voice of Firestone" and Frances Langford.

Have Gun – Will Travel (**July 26, 1959**) CBS
Weekly adult Western about a hired gunslinger, played by John Dehner. Don Ameche and Frances Langford reprise their roles as John and Blanche Bickerson for a commercial during this radio broadcast.

A Salute to Bob Hope (May 1968) AFRTS

Bob Hope's 65th birthday is celebrated with recordings from his old radio shows, including birthday greetings from Bing Crosby, Jack Benny, Jerry Colonna, Doris Day, Edgar Bergen, Jimmy Durante, Frank Sinatra, Milton Berle, George Burns, President Eisenhower and Frances Langford.

UNDATED

Swingtime (Program #40) AFRS

A thirty-minute musical offering for U.S. troops stationed overseas. Celebrity guests include Tony Romano, Mel Tormé and Frances Langford.

APPENDIX 4

Frances Langford Credits & Sources

FEATURE FILMS

"It's the busiest…snappiest musical picture of the year…packed with songs…tears and laughter!"

EVERY NIGHT AT EIGHT (1935) D: Raoul Walsh.

George Raft, Alice Faye, Patsy Kelly, Frances Langford, The Radio Rogues [Jimmy Hollywood, Eddie Bartell, Henry Taylor], Walter Catlett, Harry Barris, Herman Bing, the Ted Fio Rito Orchestra, John Dilson, Louise Carver, Charles Forsythe, Boothe Howard, Mary Jo Matthews, Florence Gill, Bud Flanagan [Dennis O'Keefe], James Miller.

Bandleader Raft turns a trio of young working women (Faye, Kelly, and Langford {as Susan Moore}) into a successful radio singing act. Musical romance adapted from the story "Three on a Mike" by Stanley Garvey. Portions filmed at Coldwater Canyon, Beverly Hills, CA.

Songs
"Take It Easy" (Jimmy McHugh; Dorothy Fields; George Oppenheimer) (sung by Faye, Langford, Kelly, Barris, Band)
"I Feel A Song Coming On" (McHugh; Oppenheimer; Fields) (sung by Faye, Langford, Kelly, Band, Chorus)
"Speaking Confidentially" (McHugh; Fields)
"Every Night At Eight" (McHugh; Fields; Oppenheimer) (sung by Faye, Langford, Kelly)
"I'm In The Mood for Love" (McHugh; Fields) (sung by Langford)
"Don't Say Goodnight" (Harry Warren; Al Dubin)
"Then You've Never Been Blue" (Ted Fio Rito; Joe Young; Frances Langford) (sung by Langford)

"Song Medley" (McHugh; Fields; Oppenheimer) (sung by Faye, Langford, Kelly)

Music by Friedrich Hollaender [Frederick Hollander], Clifford Vaughan, Sam Wineland, Paul Mertz.
Released on August 2.
(81 min.)
Walter Wanger Productions/Paramount

"Miss Langford, making her screen debut, gives promise of going places (if cast in happier roles), even without her singing."—Variety

BROADWAY MELODY OF 1936 (1935) D: Roy Del Ruth, (W.S. Van Dyke II).

Jack Benny, Eleanor Powell, Robert Taylor, Una Merkel, Sid Silvers, Buddy & Velma Ebsen. June Knight, Nick Long Jr., Robert Wildhack, Paul Harvey, Frances Langford, Harry Stockwell, Don Wilson, Irene Coleman, Beatrice Coleman, Georgina Gray, Lucille Lund, Bernadene Hayes, Rolfe Sedan, Bert Moorehouse, Luana Walters,

Patricia Gregory, Roger Edens, Lona Andre, Gertrude Astor, Jimmie Grier.

Entertainment columnist Benny has an ax to grind against Broadway producer Taylor. Langford appears as herself. Albertina Rasch choreographed the "You Are My Lucky Star" number.

Nacio Herb Brown and Arthur Freed songs
"Broadway Melody"
"You Are My Lucky Star" (AFI Song Nominee) (sung by Langford, chorus)
"I've Got A Feelin' You're Foolin'" (sung by Langford)
"Sing Before Breakfast"
"All I Do Is Dream Of You"
"On A Sunday Afternoon"
"Broadway Rhythm" (sung by Langford)
"Something's Gotta Happen Soon"
also
"The Old Folks At Home (Swanee River)" (Stephen Foster)

Academy Award (Dance Direction) Dave Gould (for "I've Got A Feelin'
    You're Foolin'" number, paired with the "Straw Hat" number from
    FOLIES BERGERE)
Academy Award Nominations
(Picture) John W. Considine Jr.
(Writing—Original Story) Moss Hart.
#8 on *Film Daily*'s '10 Best' list.
One of the 25 top-grossing films of 1935-36.
Music by Roger Edens, Alfred Newman, Edward B. Powell, Dudley
    Chambers.
Released on August 25.
(101 min./Western Electric Sound/video/laserdisc/DVD)
Metro-*Goldwyn*-Mayer

*"A line of beauty...a backfield of comics in a girls' school with Oakie and
Penner giving 100 gals lessons in love."*

COLLEGIATE (1936) D: Ralph Murphy.
    Joe Penner, Jack Oakie, Ned Sparks, Frances Langford, Betty Grable,
Lynne Overman, Betty Jane Cooper, Mack Gordon, Harry Revel, Julius
Tannen, Nora Cecil, Henry Kolker, Marjorie Moore [Reynolds], Martha
O'Driscoll, Donald Gallagher, Bob Crosby, David Sharpe.
    Oakie has an entire female student body to deal with when he
inherits a girls' school. Langford is Miss Hay. Source: 1920 play "The
Charm School" by Alice Duer Miller and Robert Milton. Remake of the
1929 film *Sweetie*. Choreography by LeRoy Prinz.

Harry Revel and Mack Gordon songs
"My Grandfather's Clock In The Hallway"
"Alma Mater"
"Bevans, Dear Bevans"
"Who Am I?"
"With My Eyes Wide Open I'm Dreaming"
"Stay As Sweet As You Are"
"You Hit The Spot" (sung by Penner, Oakie, Langford, Grable, chorus)
"Introduction To Betty Jane Cooper"
"Rhythmatic"
"I Feel Like A Feather In The Breeze"

"Learn To Be Lovely"
"Take A Number From One To Ten"
"Will I Ever Know"
"Guess Again"
also
"For He's A Jolly Good Fellow" (traditional, composer unknown)

Music by Frederick Hollander, John Leipold, Heinz Roemheld, Tom
    Satterfield.
Released on January 22.
(80 min.)
Paramount

PALM SPRINGS (1936) D: Aubrey Scotto.
    Frances Langford, [Sir] Guy Standing, Ernest Cossart, Smith Ballew,
Spring Byington, David Niven, E.E. Clive, Sterling Holloway, Grady
Sutton, Sarah Edwards, Nell Craig, Ann Doran, Lois Wilde, Jean Allen,
Fuzzy Knight, Etta McDaniel, Cyril Ring, Fred "Snowflake" Toones,
Maidel Turner.
    Englishman Standing wants to ensure that his daughter has the
proper upbringing, but he doesn't have the means—so he turns to
gambling. In the meantime, daughter Langford (as Joan Smyth) searches
for a millionaire husband, but becomes smitten with cowpoke Ballew.
Source: *Lady Smith* (novel) by Myles Connolly. Portions filmed in
Palmdale, CA.

Songs
"Will I Ever Know" (Harry Revel; Mack Gordon) (sung by Langford,
    chorus)
"I Don't Want To Make History (I Just Want To Make Love)" (Ralph
    Rainger; Leo Robin) (sung by Langford, chorus)
Hills Of Old Wyoming" (Rainger; Robin) (sung by Langford)
"Overture" featuring "I'm In The Mood For Love" (Jimmy McHugh;
    Dorothy Fields; George Oppenheimer) (sung by Langford)

Music by Charles Bradshaw, John Leipold, Boris Morros, Gerard
    Carbonara, Heinz Roemheld, Victor Young.
Released on June 5.

(74 min.)
Walter Wanger Productions/Paramount

"Corking entertainment..."—*Variety.*

"MGM's successor to **THE GREAT ZIEGFELD***"*

BORN TO DANCE (1936) D: Roy Del Ruth.
Eleanor Powell, James Stewart, Virginia Bruce, Una Merkel, Sid Silvers, Frances Langford, Raymond Walburn, Alan Dinehart, Buddy Ebsen, Juanita Quigley, Georges & Jalna, Reginald Gardiner, Barnett Parker, The Foursome [J. Marshall Smith, L. Dwight Snyder, Ray {Jay} Johnson, Del Porter], William & Joe Mandel, Leona & Naomi Keene, Charles Levison [Lane], Bobby [Robert] Watson, Charles Coleman, James Flavin, Jonathan Hale, Fuzzy Knight, Sherry Hall, Bud Flanagan [Dennis O'Keefe], Barbara Bedford, Wally Maher, Charles Trowbridge.
Performer Powell hopes for success, but right now she is the understudy for insufferable stage star Bruce. Langford is Peppy Turner (a role originally meant for Judy Garland). Portions filmed on Santa Catalina Island, CA.

Cole Porter songs
"Rolling Home"
"Rap, Tap On Wood"
"Hey, Babe, Hey" (performed by Powell {dubbed by Marjorie Lane}, Stewart, Silvers, Merkel, Langford, Ebsen, Foursome)
"Entrance Of Lucy James"
"Love Me, Love My Pekinese"
"Easy To Love" (performed by Powell/Lane, Stewart, Langford, Ebsen)
"I've Got You Under My Skin" (Academy Award Nominee) (AFI Song Nominee)
"Swingin' The Jinx Away" (sung by Langford, Ebsen, Foursome, chorus)
also
"Sidewalks Of New York" (Charles Lawlor; James W. Blake)
"Columbia, The Gem Of The Ocean" (David T. Shaw)
"The Prisoner's Song (If I Had The Wings Of An Angel)" (Guy Massey)

Additional Academy Award Nomination
(Dance Direction) Dave Gould (for "Swingin' The Jinx Away" number)
One of the 38 top-grossing films of 1936-37.
Music by Roger Edens, Alfred Newman, Edward [B.] Powell, Leo Arnaud,
      Merrill Pye.
Released on November 27.
(105 min./Western Electric Sound/video/laserdisc/DVD)
Metro-*Goldwyn*-Mayer

THE HIT PARADE/HIT PARADE OF 1937/I'LL PICK A STAR/I'LL REACH FOR A STAR (1937) D: Gus Meins.

Frances Langford, Phil Regan, Max Terhune, Edward Brophy, Louise Henry, Pert Kelton, Pierre Watkin, J. Farrell MacDonald, Monroe Owsley, Inez Courtney, William Demarest, George Givot, Sammy White, The Gentlemaniacs [Paul "Mousie" Garner, Sam Wolfe, Richard Hakins], The Tic Toc Girls [Yvonne Manoff, Mildred Winston, Barbara Johnston], Carl Hoff and the Hit Parade Orchestra, Ivy [Ivie] Anderson, Duke Ellington and His Orchestra, Eddy Duchin and His Orchestra, Molasses 'n' January [Pick & Pat, a.k.a. Pick Malone and Pat Padgett], Al Pearce, Voice of Experience [Sayle Taylor], Ed Thogersen, Oscar [Ed Platt], Elmer [Lou Fulton], Arlene Harris, William Newell, Carleton Young, Stanley Fields, Johnny Arthur.

Regan works to make Langford (as Ruth Swanson Allison) a big star to spite wealthy Henry, who left him. Various radio stars and specialty acts appear in this musical, the first entry in the **HIT PARADE** series of films. Produced by Nat Levine.

Songs
"I've Got To Be A Rug Cutter" (Duke Ellington)
"The Glory Beyond" (Alberto Colombo) (danced by Langford, Kelton)
"It Don't Mean A Thing" (Ellington)
"Along Came Pete (If It Wasn't For Pete)" (Sam H. Stept; Ned Washington)
"Hail Alma Mater" (Stept; Washington)
"Sweet Heartache" (Stept; Washington) (sung by Langford, Regan)
"Last Night I Dreamed Of You" (Stept; Washington) (sung by Langford)
"Was It Rain?" (Lou Handman; Walter Hirsch) (sung by Langford)
"Evolution" (Stept; Washington)
"I'll Reach For A Star" (Handman; Hirsch) (sung by Langford)

"Love Is Good For Anything That Ails You" (Cliff Friend; Matty Malneck)
"Happy Days Are Here Again" (Milton Ager; Jack Yellen)
"Geschichten Aus Dem Wienerwald/Wiener Blut—Medley" (Johann Strauss)

Music by Alberto Colombo, Harry Grey, Karl Hajos.
Released on April 26.
(77 min./DVD)
Republic

HOLLYWOOD HOTEL (1937) D: Busby Berkeley.
Dick Powell, Rosemary Lane, Lola Lane, Hugh Herbert, Ted Healy, Glenda Farrell, Johnnie ["Scat"] Davis, Louella Parsons, Alan Mowbray, Mabel Todd, Frances Langford, Jerry Cooper, Ken Niles, Duane Thompson, Allyn Joslyn, Grant Mitchell, Edgar Kennedy, Fritz Feld, Curt Bois, Perc Westmore, Eddie Acuff, Clinton Rosemond, William [B.] Davidson, Wally Maher, Georgia [Georgie] Cooper, Libby Taylor, Raymond Paige and His Orchestra, Benny Goodman and His Orchestra, Ronald Reagan, Gene Krupa, Susan Hayward, Lionel Hampton, Teddy Wilson, Sonny Bupp, Sid Grauman, Harry James, Carole Landis, George Offerman Jr., George O'Hanlon, Paul Whiteman and Orchestra, John Ridgely, Rosella Towne, Dale Van Sickel, Bobby Watson.
Saxophone player Powell breaks away from Goodman's band to try solo success in Hollywood, but finds the going isn't easy. Langford is Alice Crayne. Based on a popular CBS Radio program (which featured Parsons, Langford, Jerry Cooper, Niles, Thompson and the Paige orchestra). Director Berkeley also did the choreography, along with Matty King. Portions filmed at Glendale Grand Central Air Terminal in California.

Songs
"Hooray For Hollywood" (Dick [Richard A.] Whiting; Johnny Mercer) (AFI Song Nominee) (sung by Davis, Langford)
"California, Here I Come" (Joseph Meyer)
"I'm Like A Fish Out Of Water" (Whiting; Mercer)
"Silhouetted In The Moonlight" (Whiting; Mercer) (sung by Langford, Jerry Cooper)
"I've Got A Heartful Of Music" (Whiting; Mercer)
"Let That Be a Lesson To You" (Whiting; Mercer)

"Sing, Sing, Sing" (Louis Prima)

"I've Hitched My Wagon To A Star" (Whiting; Mercer)

"Ochi Tchornya (Dark Eyes)" (Russian traditional, composer unknown)

"Sing You Son-Of-A-Gun" (Whiting; Mercer) (sung by Powell, Davis, Rosemary Lane, Lola Lane, Langford, Jerry Cooper, Farrell, Healy, Todd, chorus)

"I'm A Ding Dong Daddy From Dumas" (Phil Baxter)

"Bob White (Whatcha Gonna Swing Tonight?)" (Bernard Hanighen) "Have You Got Any Castles, Baby?" (Whiting)

"Sonny Boy" (Ray Henderson; Al Jolson; B.G. 'Buddy DeSylva; Lew Brown)

"Old Black Joe" (Stephen Foster)

"Blue Moon" (Richard Rodgers)

"You Oughta Be In Pictures" (Dana Suesse)

"Old Folks At Home (Swanee River)" (Foster)

"Satan's Holiday" (Joe Venuti)

"Can't Teach My Old Heart New Tricks" (Whiting; Mercer)

Music by Heinz Roemheld, Leo F. Forbstein, Ray Heindorf, Fletcher Henderson.

Released on December 20.

(109 min./video/DVD)

Warner Brothers-First National

"The famous radio stars…answering the demand of 20,000,000 fans!"

DREAMING OUT LOUD (1940) D: Harold Young.

Chester Lauck, Norris Goff, Frances Langford, Frank Craven, Bobs Watson, Irving Bacon, Clara Blandick, Robert Wilcox, Donald Briggs, Bob [Robert] McKenzie, Phil Harris, Sheila Sheldon, Troy Brown Jr., J.P. Kelly.

Lum Edwards and Abner Peabody (Lauck, Goff), two old proprietors of a country store, use their cracker-barrel wit and backwoods wisdom to help out various folks in Pine Ridge, Arkansas. Langford plays Alice, who has a bumpy romance with Wilcox. First entry in the **LUM & ABNER** film series, based on the popular radio show. Produced by Jack William Votion and Sam Coslow.

Song
"Dreaming Out Loud" (Sam Coslow) (sung by Langford)
Music by Lucien Moraweck, Lud Gluskin.
Released on September 30.
(81 min./RCA Sound/video/DVD)
Voco Productions/RKO Radio

"It's knee-deep in gorgeous gals and gaiety!"

TOO MANY GIRLS (1940) D: George Abbott.

Lucille Ball, Richard Carlson, Ann Miller, Eddie Bracken, Frances Langford, Desi Arnaz, Hal LeRoy, Libby Bennett, Harry Shannon, Douglas Walton, Chester Clute, Tiny Person, Ivy Scott, Byron Shores, Midge Martin, Michael Alvarez, Sethma Williams, Averell Harris, Van Johnson, Jay Silverheels, Iron Eyes Cody, Grady Sutton, Chief John Big Tree, Adele Pearce [Pamela Blake].

When free-swinging heiress Ball enrolls at a New Mexico college, her father hires four football players to "keep her out of trouble." Langford is Eileen Eilers. Director Abbott co-produced this adaptation of his Broadway hit, based on a play by George Marion Jr. Choreography by LeRoy Prinz. This is the film where Lucy and Desi first met; they wed later the same year.

Richard Rodgers and Lorenz Hart songs
"Heroes In The Fall"
"You're Nearer" (sung by Langford, Miller, Bennett, Ball {dubbed by Trudy Erwin})
"Pottawatomie"
"'Cause We All Got Cake" (performed by Langford, Miller, LeRoy, Bennett, Arnaz, Bracken, chorus)
"Spic And Spanish"
"Love Never Went To College" (sung by Langford)
"Look Out" (sung by Langford, Miller, chorus)
"I Didn't Know What Time It Was"
"The Conga" (danced by Arnaz, Miller, Langford, Bracken, Bennett, Carlson, Ball, LeRoy, chorus)

Music by George Bassman.

Released on October 8.
(85 min./RCA Victor Sound/video/laserdisc/DVD)
RKO Radio

"It's in the groove! Radio and screen's brightest stars shine in this laugh-and-be-happy musicomedy tuned to your taste!"

HIT PARADE OF 1941/ROMANCE AND RHYTHM (1940) D: John H. Auer.

Kenny Baker, Frances Langford, Hugh Herbert, Mary Boland, Ann Miller, Patsy Kelly, Phil Silvers, Sterling Holloway, Donald MacBride, Barnett Parker, Franklin Pangborn, Six Hits and a Miss, Borrah Minevitch and His Harmonica Rascals, the Jan Garber Orchestra, Billy Bletcher, Veda Ann Borg, Joseph Forte, Jody Gilbert, Lionel Stander, Robert J. Wilke, Norma Varden.

Baker owns a radio station and must employ no-talent Miller in order to keep her wealthy mother's sponsorship. Baker recruits his girlfriend (Langford, as Pat Abbott) to dub Miller. Second entry in the *Hit Parade* film series. Choreography by Daniel Dare.

Songs
"Make Yourself At Home" (Jule Styne; Walter Bullock)
"Swap Shop" (Styne; Bullock)
"Trading Post Of The Air" (Styne; Bullock)
"Who Am I?" (Styne; Bullock) (Academy Award Nominee) (sung by Baker, Langford)
"Swing Low, Sweet Rhythm" (Styne; Bullock) (sung by Langford)
"In The Cool Of The Evening" (Styne; Bullock)
"Hit Parade Finale" (Styne; Bullock)
"Margie" (Con Conrad; Benny Davis; J. Russel Robinson)
"Mary Lou" (Abe Lyman; George Waggner; Robinson)
"Dinah" (Harry Akst; Sam Lewis; Joe Young)

Additional Academy Award Nomination (Music—Score) Cy Feuer.
Music by Cy Feuer, Gene Rose, Walter Scharf.
Released on October 15.
(83 min., 60 min. versions/RCA Sound)
Republic

"It's all America's choice for all-out fun!"

ALL-AMERICAN CO-ED (1941) D: LeRoy Prinz.

Frances Langford, Johnny Downs, Marjorie Woodworth, Noah Beery Jr., Esther Dale, Harry Langdon, Kent Rogers, Alan Hale Jr., Allan Lane, Joe Brown Jr., Irving Mitchell, Lillian Randolph, Carlyle Blackwell Jr., The Tanner Sisters [Mickey, Betty, Martha], Marie Windsor, Elyse Knox, Margaret Roach.

Langford stars as Virginia Collinge in this musical comedy about a college fraternity that gets involved with a beauty contest. Director Prinz co-produced with Hal Roach Jr. Entry in the *Streamliner* series of films.

Songs

"I'm A Chap With A Chip On My Shoulder" (Walter G. Samuels; Charles Newman) (sung by Langford)

"Up At The Crack Of Dawn" (Samuels; Newman)

"The Poor Farmer's Daughter" (Samuels; Newman) (sung by Langford, Downs, Tanners)

"Out Of The Silence" (Lloyd B. Norlin) (Academy Award Nominee) (sung by Langford, chorus)

Additional Academy Award Nomination (Music—Scoring of a Music Picture) Edward Ward.

Released on October 31.

(48 min./Western Electric Mirrophonic Recording/video/DVD)

Hal Roach/United Artists

"Swinging, singing screen sensation!"

SWING IT SOLDIER (1941) D: Harold Young.

Ken Murray, Frances Langford, Don Wilson, Brenda & Cobina [Blanche Stewart, Elvia Allman], Hanley Stafford, Susan Miller, Senor [Irving] Lee, Iris Adrian, Lewis Howard, Thurston Hall, Kitty O'Neil, Lew Valentine, Peter Sullivan, Tom Dugan, Kenny Stevens, Louis Da Pron, The Three Cheers, Skinnay Ennis & Orchestra, Stop, Look and Listen Trio, Riley Hill, Bert Howard, P.J. Kelly, Mel Ruick, Mickey Simpson.

Langford is expecting a baby when she is called upon to do a radio show. To fulfill her obligation, she calls in her twin sister to take her place.

Langford plays the dual roles of Evelyn Loring Waters and Patricia Loring. Reginald Le Borg directed the musical numbers. Choreography by Louis Da Pron.

Songs
"My Melancholy Baby" (G.A. Norton; Maybelle E. Watson; Ernie Burnett) (sung by Langford)
"I'm Gonna Swing My Way Up To Heaven" (Jacques Press; Eddie Cherkose) (sung by Langford, Stevens, Three Cheers, Stop, Look and Listen)
"Got Love" (Milton Rosen; Everett Carter) (sung by Langford)
"Annie Laurie" (Lady John Scott)
"Jivin' Rug Cuttin' Romeo" (Rosen; Carter)
"A Bicycle Built For Two" (Harry Dacre)
"Keep Your Thumbs Up" (Norman Berens; Jack Brooks)
"Two Hearts That Pass In The Night" (Ernesto Lecuona; Forman Brown)
"The Strings Of My Heart" (composer unknown)
"Mama Don't Allow" (Charles "Cow Cow" Davenport)
"Play Fiddle Play" (Emery Deutsch; Arthur Altman; Jack Lawrence)

Music by Charles Previn.
Released on November 7.
(66 min./Western Electric Mirrophonic Recording)
Universal

MISSISSIPPI GAMBLER/DANGER ON THE RIVER (1942) D: John Rawlins.

Kent Taylor, Frances Langford, John Litel, Shemp Howard, Claire Dodd, Wade Boteler, Douglas Fowley, Aldrich Bowker, Eddie Dunn, Harry Hayden, David Oliver, Eddie Acuff, Paul Phillips, George Reed, Alex[ander] Lockwood, Bob [Robert] Barron, Stanley Andrews, Charles Wagenheim.

Reporter Taylor takes part in chasing down criminal Litel, who has escaped to Mississippi. Langford co-stars as Beth Cornell. Choreography by Gwyneth [Gwen] Verdon.

Songs
"There Goes My Romance" (Milton Rosen; Everett Carter) (sung by Langford)

"Got Love" (Rosen; Carter) (sung by Langford)
"I'm Hittin' The High Spots" (Jimmy McHugh; Harold Adamson)

Music by Frank Skinner, Charles Previn, Ralph Freed.
Released on April 17.
(60 min.)
Universal

> *"Get ready to laugh, to sing, to shout!...For here comes Uncle Sam's*
> *Star-Spangled Yankee Doodle Dandy!"*

YANKEE DOODLE DANDY (1942) D: Michael Curtiz.

James Cagney, Joan Leslie, Walter Huston, Richard Whorf, Irene Manning, George Tobias, Rosemary DeCamp, Jeanne Cagney, Frances Langford, George Barbier, S.Z. Sakall, Walter Catlett, Douglas Croft, Eddie Foy Jr., Minor Watson, Chester Clute, Odette Myrtil, Patsy Lee Parsons, Captain Jack Young, Henry Blair, Leon Belasco, Harry Hayden, Georgia Carroll, Spencer Charters, Audrey Long, Ann Doran, Thomas Jackson, Syd Saylor, William B. Davidson, Charles Smith, Joyce Reynolds, Frank Faylen, Walter Brooke, Leslie Brooks, Wallis Clark, Tom Dugan, Pat Flaherty, James Flavin, Art Gilmore (voice), John Hamilton, William Hopper, Lon McCallister, Dolores Moran, Dave Willock, Joan Winfield.

Musical biography of the legendary, flag-waving entertainer George M. Cohan (James Cagney) who sang, danced, and composed his way to the heights of Broadway fame during the early years of the 20th century. Langford is billed as "Singer." Produced by Jack L. Warner and Hal B. Wallis, with William Cagney (James' brother) as associate. Choreography by LeRoy Prinz, Seymour Felix, and John [Jack] Boyle. Portions filmed in Washington, DC.

Songs
"Yankee Doodle Boy" (George M. Cohan) (AFI Song 71)
"Give My Regards To Broadway" (George M. Cohan) (AFI Song Nominee)
"Over There" (George M. Cohan) (sung by James Cagney, Langford, chorus)
"You're A Grand Old Flag" (George M. Cohan)
"Mary's A Grand Old Name" (George M. Cohan)
"Forty-Five Minutes From Broadway" (George M. Cohan)

"So Long, Mary" (George M. Cohan)

"Off The Record" (Richard Rodgers; Lorenz Hart)

"Harrigan" (George M. Cohan)

"At A Georgia Camp Meeting" (Kerry Mills)

"I Was Born In Virginia" (George M. Cohan)

"While Strolling Through The Park One Day" (Ed Haley)

"The Warmest Baby In The Bunch" (George M. Cohan)

"The Red, White And Blue (Columbia, The Gem Of The Ocean)" (Thomas Beckett)

"The Dancing Master" (Jerry Cohan)

"Good Luck, Johnny" (M.K. Jerome; Jack Scholl)

"Little Johnny Jones Special" (Jerome; Scholl)

"All Aboard For Old Broadway" (Jerome; Scholl)

"Oh, You Wonderful Girl" (George M. Cohan)

"Blue Skies, Gray Skies" (George M. Cohan)

"The Belle Of The Barber's Ball" (George M. Cohan)

"(I Wish I Was In) Dixie's Land" (Daniel Decatur Emmett)

"The Battle Hymn Of The Republic" (William Steffe; Julia Ward Howe)

"Auld Lang Syne" (traditional melody; Robert Burns)

"When Johnny Comes Marching Home" (Louis Lambert [Patrick Gilmore])

"America (My Country 'Tis Of Thee)" (British traditional melody; Samuel Francis Smith)

"Like The Wandering Minstrel" (George M. Cohan)

"In A Kingdom Of Our Own" (George M. Cohan) (sung by Langford)

"Love Nest" (Louis A. Hirsch; Otto Harbach) (sung by Langford)

"Nellie Kelly, I Love You" (George M. Cohan) (sung by Langford)

"The Man Who Owns Broadway" (George M. Cohan) (sung by Langford)

"Molly Malone" (George M. Cohan) (sung by Langford)

"Billie" (George M. Cohan) (sung by Langford)

"Jeepers Creepers" (Harry Warren; Johnny Mercer) (AFI Song Nominee)

"Paddock Sequence Special" (Jerome; Scholl)

"Finale Special" (Jerome; Scholl)

"Special Interlude #3" (Jerome; Scholl)

Academy Awards
    (Actor) James Cagney.

(Sound Recording) Nathan Levinson.
(Music—Scoring of a Musical Picture) Ray Heindorf, Heinz Roemheld.
Academy Award Nominations
  (Picture) Jack L. Warner, Hal B. Wallis, William Cagney.
  (Supporting Actor) Walter Huston.
  (Direction) Michael Curtiz.
  (Writing—Original Story) Robert Buckner.
  (Film Editing) George Amy.
National Board of Review Award
  (Acting) James Cagney.
New York Film Critics Circle Award
  (Best Actor) James Cagney.
#7 on *The New York Times* Ten Best list.
#3 on *Film Daily*'s Ten Best list (1943).
One of the 21 top-grossing films of 1941-42 (Box Office: $4.8 million).
Music Director: Leo F. Forbstein.
Released on May 29.
(126 min./RCA Sound/video/laserdisc/DVD/colorized/National Film Registry 1993/AFI 100)
Warner Brothers

COMBAT AMERICA (1943) D: (No director credited).
  William A. Hatcher, Philip J. Hulls, Kenneth L. Hulls, Theodore R. Geropolis, Daniel F. Stevens, Paul J. Posti, Tim Tuchet, Henry H. [Hap] Arnold, Ace Akins, Pete Provenzale, Bob Hope, Jack Pepper, Frances Langford, Tony Romano, Robert Wallace. Narrated by Clark Gable.
  Documentary focusing on the crew of a fighter-bomber during World War II. Langford appears as herself.

Music by Herbert Stothart.
(62 min./Technicolor/DVD)
U.S. Army Air Forces

"Laugh Stars! Song Stars!" Swing Stars!"

FOLLOW THE BAND/TROMBONE FROM HEAVEN (1943) D: Jean Yarbrough.

Eddie Quillan, Mary Beth Hughes, Leon Errol, Anne Rooney, Samuel S. Hinds, Bob [Robert] Mitchum, Russell Hicks, Bennie [Benny] Bartlett, Frank Coghlan Jr., Jean Ames, Frances Langford, Leo Carrillo, Ray Eberle, Alvino Rey, Skinnay Ennis & The Groove Boys, Hilo Hattie, Irving Bacon, Frank Faylen, Isabel Randolph, Robert Dudley, Paul Dubov, Frank Mitchell, Joe Bernard, Charles Sherlock, The Bombardiers, The King's Men [Ken Darby, Jon Dodson, Bud Linn, Rad Robinson], The King Sisters [Alyce, Donna, Louise, Yvonne].

A farmer who plays the trombone makes a business trip to New York and finds work in a nightclub. Langford appears as herself. Source: a *Collier's* magazine story by Richard English. Choreography by Louis Da Pron.

Songs
"What Do You Want To Make Those Eyes At Me For?" (Joseph McCarthy; Howard Johnson; James V. Monaco)
"Mush Mush (Don't Tread On The Tail Of Me Coat)" (traditional, composer unknown)
"Swingin' The Blues" (Milton Rosen; Everett Carter)
"My Melancholy Baby" (Ernie Burnett; George Norton; Maybelle Watson) (sung by Langford)
"My Devotion" (Roc Hillman; Johnny Napton)
"Rosie The Riveter" (Redd Evans; John Jacob Loeb)
"Spellbound" (Rosen; Carter)
"The Army Air Corps Song" (Robert Crawford)
"Hilo Hattie" (Harold Adamson; Don McDiarmid; Johnny Noble)
"Ain't Misbehavin'" (Thomas "Fats" Waller; Harry Brooks; Andy Razaf)
"Juanita"
"Killarney" (M.W. Balfe)

Music by Charles Previn, Frank Skinner.
Released in April.
(61 min.)
Universal

COWBOY IN MANHATTAN (1943) D: Frank Woodruff.

Frances Langford, Robert Paige, Leon Errol, Walter Catlett, Joe Sawyer, Jennifer Holt, George Cleveland, Will Wright, Dorothy Grainger [Granger], Tommy Mack, Matt McHugh, Jack Mulhall, Billy Nelson, Lorin Raker, Marek Windheim.

A songwriter wants to gain publicity for his new Broadway show and poses as a millionaire to win star Langford (as Babs Lee). Choreography by Aida Broadbent.

Milton Rosen and Everett Carter songs
"A Cowboy Is Happy"
"Whistle Your Blues To A Bluebird"
"Mr. Moon"
"Private Cowboy Jones"
"Need I Say More?"
"Got Love"

Music by H.[Hans] J. Salter, Frank Skinner.
Released on May 21.
(54 min.)
Universal

"It's your own army—in the army's own show!"

THIS IS THE ARMY (1943) D: Michael Curtiz.

George Murphy, Joan Leslie, Ronald Reagan, George Tobias, Alan Hale, Charles Butterworth, Dolores Costello, Una Merkel, Stanley Ridges, Rosemary DeCamp, Ruth Donnelly, Dorothy Peterson, Frances Langford, Gertrude Niesen, Kate Smith, Joe Louis, Alan Anderson, Ezra Stone, Tom D'Andrea, James Burrell, Ross Elliott, Alan Manson, John Prinze Mendes, Julie Oshins, Earl Oxford, Robert Shanley, Philip Truex, James MacColl, Herbert Anderson, Ralph Magelssen, Tilestone Perry, John Cook Jr., Larry Weeks, The Allon Trio, Ross Ford, Irving Berlin, Ilka Gruning, Doodles Weaver, Captain Jack Young, Patsie Moran, Irving Bacon, Warner Anderson, Frank Coghlan Jr., John Daheim, Victor Moore, Ernest Truex, Jimmy Conlin, Henry Jones, Richard Crane, Richard Farnsworth, John James, Bill Kennedy, Gary Merrill, Gene Nelson, Hayden Rorke, Arthur Space, Pierre Watkin.

Irving Berlin ("Medal of Merit" winner) musical about father-and-son show business producers (Murphy, Reagan), who put on patriotic extravaganzas during two wars. Langford appears as herself. Source: "Yip, Yip Yaphank" and "This Is The Army" (plays) by Irving Berlin. Choreography by LeRoy Prinz and Robert Sidney. Restored in 1991.

Irving Berlin songs
"For Your Country And My Country"
"My Sweetie"
"Poor Little Me, I'm On K.P."
"We're On Our Way To France"
"God Bless America" (AFI Song Nominee)
"What Does He Look Like, That Boy Of Mine?" (sung by Langford, ensemble)
"This Is The Army, Mr. Jones"
"I'm Getting Tired So I Can Sleep"
"Mandy"
"The Army's Made A Man Out Of Me"
"Ladies Of The Chorus"
"That's What The Well-Dressed Man In Harlem Will Wear"
"How About A Cheer For The Navy"
"I Left My Heart At The Stage Door Canteen"
"With My Head In The Clouds"
"American Eagles"
"Oh, How I Hate To Get Up In the Morning"
"This Time (Is The Last Time)"
"Alexander's Ragtime Band"
"Hostesses Of The Stage Door Canteen"
"Good-Bye France"
"I Can Always Find A Little Sunshine In The YMCA"
"Dressed Up To Win"
also
"The Girl I Left Behind Me" (traditional, composer unknown)
"Hail To The Chief" (James Sanderson)

Academy Award
(Music—Scoring of a Musical Picture) Ray Heindorf.

Academy Award Nominations
 (Art Direction-Interior Decoration—Color) John Hughes, John
 Koenig; George J. Hopkins)
 (Sound Recording) Nathan Levinson.
#4 on *Film Daily*'s Ten Best list.
One of the 24 top-grossing films of 1942-43 (Box Office: $8,301,000).
Additional Music by Max Steiner, Leo F. Forbstein.
Released on July 29.
(121 min./RCA Sound/Technicolor/video/DVD)
Warner Brothers

NEVER A DULL MOMENT (1943) D: Edward Lilley.
 The Ritz Brothers [Al, Harry, Jimmy], Frances Langford, Mary Beth
Hughes, Stuart Boyd Crawford, George Zucco, Elisabeth Risdon, Franklin
Pangborn, Jack La Rue, Sammy Stein, The Rogers Dancers [Dorothy
Rogers, George Rogers, Don Kramer], Grace Poggi & Igor, Barbara Brown,
Douglas Wood, Charles Jordan, Lorin Raker, John Sheehan, Eddie Dunn,
Ruby Dandridge, George Chandler, James Eagles, Milton Kibbee, Gene
O'Donnell, Jan Wiley, Spec O'Donnell.
 The Ritzes play gangsters in a nightclub act and end up trying to
avert a real robbery. Langford is Julie Russell.

Songs
"My Blue Heaven" (Walter Donaldson; George Whiting) (sung by
 Langford)
"Sleepy Time Gal" (Richard A. Whiting; Ange Lorenzo; Raymond B.
 Egan; Joseph E. Alden)
"Hello" (Eddie Cherkose; David Rose; Jacques Press)
"Yakimboomba" (Cherkose; Rose; Press)
"Once You Find Your Guy" (Cherkose; Rose)
"Mr. Five By Five" (Gene de Paul; Don Raye)
Music by Hans J. Salter, Charles Previn, Paul Sawtell, Frank Skinner, Ted
 Cain.
Released on November 19.
(60 min.)
Universal

"...It's a drama steeplechase set to music."

CAREER GIRL (1944) D: Wallace Fox.
Frances Langford, Edward Norris, Iris Adrian, Craig Woods, Linda Brent, Alec Craig, Ariel Heath, Lorraine Krueger, Gladys Blake, Charles Judels, Charles Williams, Renee White [Helms], Marion [Marcy] McGuire, Bess Flowers, Eddie Kane, Larry Steers, Horace B. Carpenter, Jack Chefe.
Langford (as Joan Terry) hopes to become a successful actress and follows her dream to New York, but her fiancé stands in her way.

Songs
"That's How The Rumba Began" (Morey Amsterdam; Tony Romano) (sung by Langford)
"Some Day" (Amsterdam; Romano) (sung by Langford)
"Blue In Love Again" (Michael Breen; Sam Neuman) (sung by Langford)
"A Dream Came True" (Breen; Neuman) (sung by Langford)
"Buck Dance" (traditional, composer unknown)

Music by David Chudnow, Rudy Schrager.
Released on January 11.
(69 min./video/DVD)
PRC

"You'll go on a musical spree!"

DIXIE JAMBOREE (1944) D: Christy Cabanne.
Frances Langford, Guy Kibbee, Eddie Quillan, Charles Butterworth, Fifi D'Orsay, Lyle Talbot, Frank Jenks, Almira Sessions, Joe Devlin, Louise Beavers, Ben Carter and His Choir, Gloria Jetter, Edward [Ward] Shattuck, Ethel Shattuck, Anthony Warde, Angel [Angelo] Cruz, Eddie Kane, Emmett Lynn, Ralph Peters.
Langford stars as Susan Jackson in this opus about two criminals (Talbot, Jenks) aboard a riverboat attempting to profit from its cargo of whiskey.

Michael Breen and Sam Neuman songs
"(You Ain't Right With The Lord) Repent, Brother, Repent"

"Dixie Showboat" (sung by Langford)
"If It's A Dream" (sung by Langford)
"No, No, No!"
"Big Stuff" (sung by Langford)

Music by Dave [David] Chudnow, Rudy Schrager.
Released on August 15.
(80 min./Western Electric Mirrophonic Recording/video/DVD)
PRC

GIRL RUSH (1944) D: Gordon Douglas.
Wally Brown & Alan Carney, Frances Langford, Vera Vague [Barbara Jo Allen], Robert Mitchum, Paul Hurst, Patti Brill, Sarah Padden, Cyrus W. Kendall, John Merton, Diana King, Rita Corday, Elaine Riley, Rosemary La Planche, Daun Kennedy, Virginia Belmont, Michael Vallon, Sherry Hall, Kernan Cripps, Wheaton Chambers, Chili Williams, Dale Van Sickel, Ernie Adams, Bobby Barber, Kenneth Terrell, Bud Osborne, Byron Foulger, Bert LeBaron, Lee Phelps, Paul Newlan, George Magrill.
A pair of vaudevillians (Brown, Carney) try to strike gold at Sutter's Mill in 1849. When they fail, the boys decide to bring in a bunch of showgirls, divert the prospectors, and fill their pockets. Langford plays Flo Daniels. From the story "Petticoat Fever" by Laszlo Vadnay and Aladar Laszlo. Choreography by Charles O'Curran.

Songs
"(When I'm) Walking Arm In Arm With Jim" (Lew Pollack; Harry Harris)
    (sung by Langford)
"Annabella's Bustle" (Pollack; Harris) (sung by Langford, chorus)
"If Mother Could Only See Us Now" (Pollack; Harris)
"Rainbow Valley" (Pollack; Harris) (sung by Langford)
"Oh! Susanna" (Stephen Foster)
"Sobre Las Olas (Over The Waves)" (Juventino Rosas)
"Polly Wolly Doodle" (traditional, composer unknown)
"(I Wish I Was In) Dixie's Land" (Daniel Decatur Emmett)
"Gwine To Rune All Night (De Camptown Races)" (Foster)
"Old Folks At Home (Swanee River)" (Foster)

Music by Leigh Harline, Paul Sawtell, Roy Webb, Constantin Bakaleinikoff, Gene Rose.
Released on October 21.
(65 min./RCA Sound/Rated [TV-G]/video)
RKO Radio

RADIO STARS ON PARADE (1945) D: Leslie Goodwins.

Wally Brown & Alan Carney, Frances Langford, Ralph Edwards, Skinnay Ennis and His Band, Don Wilson, Tony Romano, Rufe Davis, Robert Clarke, Sheldon Leonard, Max Wagner, Ralph Peters, The Town Criers, The Cappy Bara Boys, Jason Robards [Sr.], Gino Corrado, Myrna Dell, Sam Harris, George Magrill, Emory Parnell, Jack Rice, Ray Walker, Harry Woods.

Two bumbling talent agents (Brown, Carney) take on client Langford (as Sally Baker), who wants to become a star on radio. Matters are complicated when a mobster enters the picture.

Songs
"Don't Believe Everything You Dream" (Jimmy McHugh; Harold Adamson) (sung by Langford)
"Can't Get Out Of This Mood" (McHugh; Frank Loesser) (sung by Langford)
"My Shining Hour" (Harold Arlen; Johnny Mercer) (sung by Langford)
"That Old Black Magic" (Arlen; Mercer) (AFI Song Nominee) (sung by Langford)
"My Grandfather's Clock" (Henry Clay Work)
"I Couldn't Sleep A Wink Last Night" (McHugh; Adamson)
"I'm The Sound Effects Man" (Jock [Jack Rock]; George Gray)
"Come Out, Come Out, Wherever You Are" (Jule Styne; Sammy Cahn)
"Heavenly, Isn't It?" (Harry Revel; Mort Greene)

Music by Roy Webb, Constantin Bakaleinikoff, Gene Rose.
Released on August 1.
(70 min./RCA Sound)
RKO Radio

PEOPLE ARE FUNNY (1946) D: Sam White.

Jack Haley, Helen Walker, Rudy Vallee, Ozzie Nelson, Phillip Reed, Bob Graham, Barbara Roche, Art Linkletter, Frances Langford, Clara Blandick, Roy Atwell, Ann Jenkins, Wheaton Chambers, Casey Johnson, Rosarita Varela, Lillian Molieri, The Vagabonds, Joe DeRita.

Announcer Haley has an idea for a radio show and tries to sell it to producer Reed and sponsor Vallee. Fictionalized account of how the real *People Are Funny* (created by John Guedel and hosted by Linkletter) got on the air. Langford appears as herself. Choreography by Jack Crosby. Produced by William H. Pine and William C. Thomas, along with director White.

Songs
"I'm In The Mood For Love" (Jimmy McHugh; Dorothy Fields) (sung by
    Langford, chorus)
"Every Hour On The Hour" (Duke Ellington; Don George)
"Hey, Jose (Que Sera)" (Pepe and Tito Guizar; Jay Livingston; Ray Evans)
"Angelina" (Allan Roberts; Doris Fisher)
"The Old Square Dance Is Back Again" (Don Reid; Henry Tobias)
"Alouette" (French-Canadian traditional, composer unknown; English
    lyrics by Rudy Vallee)
"Chuck-A-Luckin'" (Archie Gottler; Jay Milton; Walter G.G. Samuels)
"Cielito Lindo" (C. Fernandez)

Music by David Chudnow, Rudy Schrager.
Released on January 11.
(94 min./Western Electric Mirrophonic Recording/video/DVD)
Pine-Thomas/Paramount

THE BAMBOO BLONDE (1946) D: Anthony Mann.

Frances Langford, Ralph Edwards, Russell Wade, Iris Adrian, Richard Martin, Jane Greer, Glenn Vernon, Paul Harvey, Regina Wallace, Jean Brooks, Tom [Tommy] Noonan, Dorothy Vaughan, Jason Robards [Sr.], Eddie Acuff, Robert Clarke, Bruce Edwards, Harry Harvey, Robert Karnes, Nan Leslie, Walter Reed.

After a brief romance with Langford (as Louise Anderson), war pilot Wade paints her picture on the side of his B-29. Subsequently, the plane and its crew become the terror of the Pacific—downing many

Japanese aircraft. Source: "Chicago Lulu" (story) by Wayne Whittaker. Choreography by Charles O'Curran.

Lew Pollack and Mort Greene songs
"Good For Nothing But Love" (sung by Langford)
"Dreaming Out Loud" (sung by Langford)
"Moonlight Over The Islands" (sung by Langford, chorus)
"Along About Evening" (sung by Langford, Harvey, Edwards,
        Adrian, Wallace)
Music by Constantin Bakaleinikoff.
Released on July 15.
(68 min./RCA Sound/DVD)
RKO Radio

"A musical love story in laughtime!"

BEAT THE BAND (1947) D: John H. Auer.
    Frances Langford, Ralph Edwards, Philip Terry, June Clayworth, Mabel Paige, Andrew Tombes, Donald MacBride, Mira McKinney, Harry Harvey, Grady Sutton, Gene Krupa and His Band, Ellen Corby, Frank Darien, Tommy Noonan.
    Ex-serviceman Terry wants to re-form the band he left during the war, but comes up short of funds. He strikes upon the notion to become a voice teacher, and finds romance with pupil Langford (as Ann Rogers). Source: Broadway show by George Abbott, Johnny Green, and George Marion Jr.

Songs
"I Couldn't Sleep A Wink Last Night" (Jimmy McHugh; Harold Adamson)
"I've Got My Fingers Crossed" (Leigh Harline; Mort Greene) (sung by
        Langford)
"Kissin' Well" (Harline; Greene) (sung by Langford)
"Shadow Rhapsody" (instrumental) (Gene Krupa)
"I'm In Love" (Harline; Greene) (sung by Langford)
"Drum Boogie" (Krupa)
"Dr. Gillespie" (Ernie Finkel)
"Steam Is On The Beam" (Johnny Green; George Marion Jr.)

Music by Leigh Harline.
Released on February 19.
(67 min.)
RKO Radio

"For your all-time good time!"

MELODY TIME (1948) D: Clyde Geronimi, Wilfred Jackson, Hamilton Luske, Jack Kinney.

Roy Rogers, Trigger, Dennis Day (voice), The Andrews Sisters [Patty, Maxene, Laverne], Fred Waring and His Pennsylvanians, Freddy Martin and His Orchestra, Ethel Smith, Frances Langford (voice), The Dinning Sisters [Lou, Jean, Ginger], Bob Nolan and the Sons of the Pioneers, Jack Fina, Bobby Driscoll, Luana Patten. Narrated by Buddy Clark.

Animated film comprised of seven stories. Langford is among those who provide vocals.

1. "Once Upon a Wintertime"—The romance of a boy and girl in the cold months.
2. "Bumble Boogie"—A jazzy rendition underscores the tale of a bumblebee plagued by musical notes and instruments.
3. "Johnny Appleseed"—The famous folk tale of an itinerant planter.
4. "Little Toot"—A small tugboat proves to be a big hero.
5. "Trees"—Animated telling of the famous poem by Joyce Kilmer.
6. "Blame It on the Samba"—Jose Carioca, Donald Duck, and the Aracuan Bird cavort.
7. "Pecos Bill"—The larger-than-life frontier hero performs some wild western wooing when he conquers Sluefoot.

Songs
"Melody Time" (Ben Benjamin; George David Weiss)
"Once Upon A Wintertime" (Bobby Worth; Ray Gilbert) (sung by Langford)
"Flight Of The Bumblebee" (Nicolai Rimsky-Korsakov; re-arranged as "Bumble Boogie" by Jack Fina)
"Johnny Appleseed/The Apple Song" (Walter Kent; Kim Gannon)
"Little Toot" (Allie Wrubel)
"Trees" (Oscar Rasbach; Joyce Kilmer)

"Blame It On The Samba" (Ernesto Nazareth; Ray Gilbert)
"Pecos Bill" (Eliot Daniel; Johnny Lange)
"The Lord Is Good To Me" (Kent; Gannon)
"The Pioneer Song" (Kent; Gannon)
"Apanhei-Te-Cavaquinho" (Nazareth; Gilbert)
"Blue Shadows On The Trail" (Daniel; Lange)
"Sluefoot Sue" (Bob Nolan; Tim Spencer; Erdman Penner; Winston
    Hibler)

Music by Paul J. Smith, Ken Darby, Al Sack, Vic Schoen.
Released on May 27.
(75 min./RCA Sound/Technicolor/video/DVD)
Walt Disney Productions/RKO Radio

"Terrific trigger thrills…in a terror-stricken town!"

DEPUTY MARSHAL (1949) D: William Berke.

Jon Hall, Frances Langford, Dick Foran, Julie Bishop, Joe Sawyer, Russell Hayden, Clem Bevans, Vince Barnett, Mary Gordon, Kenne Duncan, Stanley Blystone, Roy Butler, Wheaton Chambers, Forrest Taylor, Tom Greenway, Ray Jones, Cliff Taylor.

Hall has his hands full chasing bank robbers and thwarting land-grabbers when romance comes along in the form of lovely Langford (as Janet Masters). Western taken from a novel by Charles Heckermann. Portions filmed at Iverson Ranch in Chatsworth, CA.

Songs
"Levis, Plaid Shirt And Spurs" (Irving Bibo; John Stephens) (sung by
    Langford)
"Hideout In Hidden Valley" (Bibo; Stephens) (sung by Langford)

Music by David Chudnow, Mahlon Merrick.
Released on October 28.
(72 min./Garutso Balanced Lens [3-D]/video/DVD)
Lippert

PURPLE HEART DIARY (1951) D: Richard Quine.

Frances Langford, Judd Holdren, Ben Lessy, Tony Romano, Aline Towne, Brett King, Warren Mills, Larry Stewart, Joel Marston, Richard Grant, Rory Mallinson, Selmer Jackson, Lyle Talbot, Douglas Banks, William R. Klein, Harry Guardino, Marshall Reed, Steve Pendleton, George Offerman Jr., William Bryant. Archive footage of Al Jolson.

Langford appears as herself in the war drama of a USO contingent sent overseas to entertain G.I.s. She also has time to facilitate a romance between severely wounded soldier King and nurse Towne. Adapted from Hearst newspaper columns written by Langford. Produced by Sam Katzman.

Songs
"Hold Me In Your Arms" (Tony Romano; Barbara Hayden; Johnny Bradford) (sung by Langford)
"Hi, Fellow Tourists" (Romano; Hayden; Bradford) (sung by Langford)
"Bread And Butter Woman" (Allan Roberts; Lester Lee) (sung by Langford)
"Anywhere" (Jule Styne; Sammy Cahn)
"Tattletale Eyes" (Romano; Bradford) (sung by Langford)
"Where Are You From" (Romano; Hayden; Bradford) (sung by Langford)

Music by Ross DiMaggio, George Antheil, Sidney Cutner, Miklos Rozsa, Marlin Skiles, Victor Young.
Released on November 12.
(73 min./sepiatone/video/DVD)
Columbia

"It was a time that changed the world. And one man put it to music."

THE GLENN MILLER STORY (1954) D: Anthony Mann.

James Stewart, June Allyson, Henry [Harry] Morgan, Charles Drake, George Tobias, Barton MacLane, Sig Ruman, Irving Bacon, James Bell, Kathleen Lockhart, Katharine [Katherine] Warren, Frances Langford, Louis Armstrong, Ben Pollack, Gene Krupa, Barney Bigard, James Young, Marty Napoleon, Arvell Shaw, Cozy Cole, Babe Russin, Dayton Lummis, Marion Ross, Kevin Corcoran, Phil Garris, The Modernaires [Alan Copeland, Hal Dickinson, Fran Scott], Ruth Hampton, Damian O'Flynn,

Lionel Hampton, Carleton Young, William Challee, Steve Pendleton, Harry Harvey, Dick Ryan, Hal K. Dawson, The Mellomen [Bob Hamlin, Bill Lee, Thurl Ravenscroft, Max Smith], The Rolling Robinsons, Lisa Gaye.

Hollywood-style biography of the trombonist who became one of America's top bandleaders, until he was lost during World War II. Langford appears as herself. Choreography by Kenny Williams. Portions filmed at the following California locations: 3rd Street Tunnel Stairway, Los Angeles; Angel's Flight Railway, Bunker Hill, Los Angeles; Clay Valley, Los Angeles; and Santa Monica Pier. Portions also filmed at the following Colorado locations: Boulder and Lowry Air Force Base, Denver.

Songs
"Basin Street Blues" (Spencer Williams)
"Over The Rainbow" (Harold Arlen; E.Y. Harburg) (AFI Song 1)
"I Know Why" (Harry Warren; Mack Gordon)
"A String Of Pearls" (Jerry Gray; Eddie DeLang)
"Pennsylvania 6-5000" (Gray; Carl Sigman)
"Tuxedo Junction" (Erskine Hawkins; William Johnson; Julian Dash; Buddy Feyne)
"St. Louis Blues" (W.C. Handy) (arrangement by Glenn Miller)
"In The Mood" (Joe Garland; Andy Razaf)
"Chattanooga Choo Choo" (Warren; Gordon) (sung by Langford, Modernaires, Band) (AFI Song Nominee)
"American Patrol" (F.W. Meacham)
"Little Brown Jug" (Joseph Winner)
"Too Little Time" (Henry Mancini)
"At Last" (Warren; Gordon)
"Moonlight Serenade" (Glenn Miller; Mitchell Parish)
"Good Night, Ladies" (traditional, composer unknown)
"Santa Lucia" (Teodoro Cottrau)
"Bridal Chorus" from "Lohengrin" (Richard Wagner)
"Bidin' My Time" (George & Ira Gershwin)
"Elmer's Tune" (Elmer Albrecht)
"Adios" (Enrico Madriguera)
"National Emblem March" (Edwin Eugene Bagley)
"God Rest Ye Merry Gentlemen" (traditional, composer unknown)
"Deck The Halls With Boughs Of Holly" (traditional, composer unknown)
"Looking At The World Through Rose Colored Glasses" (Tommy Malie; Jimmy Steiger)

Academy Award
    (Sound Recording) Leslie I. Carey.
Academy Award Nominations
    (Writing—Story and Screenplay) Valentine Davies, Oscar Brodney.
    (Music—Scoring of a Musical Picture) Joseph Gershenson, Henry Mancini.
Screen Directors Guild of America Award Nomination
    (Best Director) Anthony Mann.
Screen Writers Guild of America Award Nomination
    (Best Written Musical) Valentine Davies, Oscar Brodney.
British Academy of Film and Television Arts Award Nomination
    (Best Foreign Actor) James Stewart (USA).
"Best Film of the Year"—*New York Times.*
#9 on *Film Daily*'s "Ten Best" list.
One of the 25 top-grossing films of 1953-54.
Released on January 8.
(116 min./Western Electric Recording/Technicolor/video/laserdisc/ DVD)
Universal-International

SHORT SUBJECTS

THE SUBWAY SYMPHONY (1932) D: (No director credited).
    Joan Abbott, Charles Bennington, Frank Hazard, Frances Langford, The Dave Gould Dancers, The Rhythm Boys.
    The New York subway becomes a lively place to be when musical entertainers show up. Langford sings. Choreography by Dave Gould.

Songs
"Was That The Human Thing To Do?" (Sammy Fain; Joe Young)
"It Cost Me Just A Nickel" (Fain; Irving Kahal)
"Rhythm Of The Wheels" (Ruebens)
"Doing The Subway"
"China Boy" (Phil Boutelje; Dick Winfree)
"Collegiate" (Nat Bonx; Moe Jaffe)
"Nobody's Sweetheart Now" (Billy Meyers; Elmer Schoebel; Gus Kahn; Ernie Erdman)

Released in February.
(18 min.)
Vitaphone/Warner Brothers

RAMBLING 'ROUND RADIO ROW #2 (1932) D: Jerry Wald.

Jerry Wald, The Happiness Boys [Billy Jones, Ernie Hare], The Funnyboners, Ted Husing, Smith Ballew, Frances Langford, Les Reis & Artie Dunn, Arthur Tracy, Lois Wilson, Jacques Renard, Freddie Rich, Jack Denny, Meyer Davis.

The Happiness Boys try to escape performing at a party by watching other radio acts. Langford and Ballew trade love songs.

Songs
"Bound For The Bronx" (Sammy Fain)
"Bye, Bye, Blackbird" (Ray Henderson; Mort Dixon)
"Deep In Your Eyes" (Harry Warren; Dixon)
"Hello, My Lover, Goodbye" (Johnny Green; Edward Heyman) (sung by
    Langford)
"Martha, Martha, Tu Sparigis" (Friedrich von Flotow)
"Where The Blue Of The Night (Meets The Gold Of The Day)" (Fred E.
    Ahlert; Roy Turk)
"Hot Tamales" (Marion Sunshine)
"Humming To Myself" (Fain; Herb Magidson)
"Music Hath Charms" (Harry Barris; Sam M. Lewis)
"It Was So Beautiful" (Barris; Arthur Freed)
"Sun's In My Heart"

Released in July.
(10 min.)
Vitaphone/Warner Brothers

SUNKIST STARS AT PALM SPRINGS (1936) D: Roy Rowland.

Edmund Lowe, The Fanchonettes, The Downey Sisters, [Peter] Lind Hayes, Bob [Robert] Benchley, Jackie Coogan, Frankie Darro, Dick Foran, Betty Furness, Betty Grable, Walter Huston, Buster Keaton, Fuzzy Knight, Frances Langford, Sir Guy Standing, Claire Trevor, Johnny Weissmuller, Vince Barnett, Ricardo Cortez, Hugh Herbert, Jack Mulhall, Mary Stewart.

The 48 national winners of the Lucky Stars Dance Contest—one from each state—interact with the stars as they visit Palm Springs. Langford sings for the assembled crowd.

Songs
"Wah! Hoo!" (Cliff Friend)
"You Are My Lucky Star" (Nacio Herb Brown; Arthur Freed)
"Broadway Rhythm" (Brown; Freed) (sung by Langford)
"Turkey In The Straw" (traditional, composer unknown)
"Aloha Oe" (Queen Liliuokalani)
"(I Wish I Was In) Dixie's Land" (Daniel Decatur Emmett)
"Minnehaha" (composer unknown)
"Semper Fidelis" (John Philip Sousa)

Released on August 6.
(20 min./Technicolor/DVD)
Metro-*Goldwyn*-Mayer

PICTURE PEOPLE NO. 4: STARS DAY OFF (1941) D: M. Clay Adams.
Joan Carroll, Jon Hall, Jack Marmory, Frances Langford, Marian Marsh, Felix Mills, Edward Norris, Shirley Ross, Henry Wilcoxon, Joan Woodbury.
A peek at some off-screen activities of movie people. Carroll and skating instructor Marmory go through some figure-eights. Ross, Langford, Hall, and Mills go out to sea; Ross and Langford check out the boat and its equipment. Woodbury, Wilcoxon, Marsh, and Norris stay ashore to race model boats.

Released on December 6.
(9 min./RCA Sound)
RKO Radio

PICTURE PEOPLE NO. 10: HOLLYWOOD AT HOME (1942) D: M. Clay Adams.
Bud Abbott & Lou Costello, Alfred Hitchcock, Frances Langford.
A look, off-screen, of various stars (including Langford). Features archive footage of Carole Lombard.

Released on May 23.
(9 min.)
RKO Radio

HEDDA HOPPER'S HOLLYWOOD NO. 4 (1942) D: Herbert Moulton.
Hedda Hopper, Freddie Bartholomew, Bobby Breen, Leo Carrillo, Joan Carroll, Cora Sue Collins, Jerry Colonna, Skinnay Ennis, Edith Fellows, Bob Hope, Elsie Janis, Jim [James J.] Jeffries, Bobby Jordan, Frances Langford, Butch & Buddy [Billy Lenhart, Kenneth Brown], Gloria Lloyd, Peggy Lloyd, Sidney Miller, Dickie Moore, Juanita Quigley, Gene Reynolds, Charles Smith, Bobs Watson, Jane Withers.
Hopper hosts a parade of juvenile movie players, plus members of Bob Hope's radio show (Colonna, Langford, Ennis) and others.

Released on June 19.
(10 min./Western Electric Mirrophonic Recording)
Paramount

MEMO FOR JOE (1944) D: Richard Fleischer.
Quentin Reynolds, Joe E. Brown, Gary Cooper, Marlene Dietrich, Bob Hope, Frances Langford, John Wayne.
Featurette showing what the American Community Chest charity drives contribute to the allied war effort. Langford appears as herself.

Released on August 10.
(10 min.)
National War Fund/U.S. Public Relations Department of Community Chests & Councils/War Activities Committee of the Motion Picture Industry/RKO Radio

SCREEN SNAPSHOTS SERIES 25, NO. 7: HOLLYWOOD VICTORY SHOW (1946) D: Ralph Staub.
Jerry Colonna, Harry Crocker, Kay Kyser, Frances Langford, Victor Mature, Tony Romano, Cesar Romero, Sabu.
Tinseltown celebrates the end of World War II with the stars (including Langford).

Released on March 15.
(9 min.)
Columbia

STAGE APPEARANCES

"HERE GOES THE BRIDE" (1931) D: Edward Clarke Lilley.

Bobby Clark & Paul McCullough, Eric Blore, Coletta Ryan, Grace Brinkley, Dudley Clements, Victoria Cummings, Dorothy Dare, Paul Frawley, John Gallaudet, Pauline Gaskins, Charlotte Homann, Frances Langford.

Langford plays Rose in this musical comedy about divorce, featuring funnymen Clark & McCullough. Choreography by Russell Markert.

Songs
"The Inside Story" (John W. [Johnny] Green; Edward Heyman)
"Remarkable People We" (Richard Myers; Heyman)
"My Sweetheart 'Tis Of Thee" (Green; Heyman)
"Shake Well Before Using" (Green; Heyman)
"We Know Reno" (Green; Heyman)
"Well, You See" (Green; Heyman)
"What's The Difference" (Green; Heyman)
"One Second Of Sex" (Myers; Heyman)
"Hello, My Lover, Goodbye" (Green; Heyman) (sung by Langford, ensemble)
"It's My Nature" (Green; Heyman)
"It Means So Little To You" (Green; Heyman)
"Music In My Fingers" (Myers; Heyman) (sung by Langford, ensemble)

Music by Adolph Deutsch, Conrad Salinger.
Run: November 3 to November 7.
(7 performances)
Peter Arno/Chanin's 46ᵗʰ Street Theatre (New York City)

"THE PURE IN HEART" (1934) D: Edward Massey.

Joseph Allenton, James Bell, Larry Bolton, Ruth Bond, C.H. Davis, Peggy Dell, Peter Donald Jr., Ara Gerald, Dorothy Hall, Frances Langford, Mary Philips, Tom Powers, Harold Vermilyea.

Drama with Langford as "a singer."

Music by Richard Myers.
Run: March 20 to circa March 25.
(7 performances)
Richard Aldrich, Alfred De Liagre Jr./Longacre Theatre (New York City)

TELEVISION APPEARANCES

"WXYZ INAUGURAL PROGRAM" (ABC) (Special) October 9, 1948.
Host: Georgie Price. The Paul Whiteman Orchestra.
    The Detroit, Michigan, TV station goes on the air. A speech by Gov. Kim Sigler, followed by a variety show.
    Frances Langford, Paul and Grace Hartman, Sugar Chile Robinson.

WINDOW ON THE WORLD (DuMont) Early 1949.
The Merle Kendrick Orchestra.
    Variety acts from around the globe with film clips of various countries. Frances Langford is a guest.

"ALL-STAR THANKSGIVING DAY SHOW" (NBC)(Special) November 24, 1949.
    A holiday treat presented by Elgin-American, makers of watches and compacts. Ninety minutes of variety with Milton Berle, George Jessel, The Ritz Brothers, Frances Langford, The Charioteers, Mata and Hari, Phil Regan, and others. The Charles Sanford Orchestra.

CAVALCADE OF STARS (DuMont) January 14, 1950.
Host: Jack Carter. Announcer: Jimmy Blaine. The Sammy Spear/Charlie Spear Orchestra.
    Comedy-variety with guests: vocalist Frances Langford; comedian Jack Leonard; the dancing Step Brothers; Ladd Lyon; Bobby Whaling.

THE JACK CARTER SHOW (NBC) March 18, 1950.
Star: Jack Carter. Vocalist: Don Richards. Dancer: Bill Callahan. The Lou Breese Orchestra.
    Variety with guests the dancing Step Brothers; comedian Benny Baker; comedy team Smith & Dale; and singer Frances Langford.

THE ED WYNN SHOW (CBS) May 18, 1950 (West Coast), June 6, 1950 (East Coast).
Star: Ed Wynn. Announcer: Bob Lemond. The Lud Gluskin Orchestra.
   Comedy-variety with guests Frances Langford and Fred Sanborn. *Broadcast live from Hollywood with kinescopes sent to the East for later telecast.*

CAVALCADE OF STARS (DuMont) August 19, 1950.
Host/Star: Jackie Gleason. Regulars: Art Carney, Pert Kelton. The June Taylor Dancers. Announcer: Jimmy Blaine. The Sammy Spear Orchestra.
   Guest Frances Langford sings and plays Lady Lou in a Wild West sketch. Also, comic pianist Victor Borge; singer Don Richards; and dancer Gloria Gilbert.

STAR TIME (DuMont)(Series) September 5, 1950 to February 27, 1951.
   Musical variety featuring the verbal antics of the Bickersons.
   Cast

Host/John Bickerson	Lew Parker
Vocalist/Blanche Bickerson	Frances Langford
Regular	Reginald Gardiner
	(10/3/50-2/27/51)
Dancer	Kathryn Lee
Announcer	John Conte
	(10/3/50-2/27/51)
Orchestra	The Benny Goodman Sextet

D'Artega
Approx. 26 episodes.

THE FRIGIDAIRE COMEDY HOUR: MICHAEL TODD'S REVUE (NBC) October 29, 1950.
Host: Bobby Clark. Announcer: Nelson Case. The Tom Jones Orchestra.
   Bobby presents a comic skit based on "The Shooting of Dan McGrew." Guests include sportscaster Mel Allen; singer Frances Langford; tennis star Gussie Moran; jugglers the Peiro Brothers; and comedians the Albins.

STAR OF THE FAMILY (CBS) December 1, 1950.
Host: Morton Downey [Sr.]. The Carl Hoff Orchestra.
   Morton interviews relatives of famous guest celebrities before bringing out each guest to entertain. Singer-actor Dick Haymes; the

musical Hoosier Hot Shots; dance team of Andre & Bonnie; actor Jon Hall and his wife Frances Langford; comedian Ken Murray.

THE JACK CARTER SHOW (NBC) January 27, 1951.
Star: Jack Carter. Vocalist: Don Richards. The Harry Sosnik Orchestra.
    Comedy with songs. Ben Blue is guest MC.
    Roberta Lee, Frances Langford, Sid Fields, The Whipporwills.

THE KEN MURRAY SHOW (CBS) March 3, 1951.
Stars: Ken Murray, Darla Hood, Laurie Anders, Joe Wong, Tony Labriola, Jack Mulhall, Betty Lou Walters, Joe Besser. Vocalists: Art Lund, The Enchanters. Announcer: Nelson Case. The David Broekman Orchestra.
    A "Salute to the Marines" features service personnel wearing period costumes and a re-enactment of the flag-raising on Iwo Jima.
    Jon Hall, Frances Langford, Rosie the Bear, Lovey the Deer, The Australian Woodchoppers, The Royal Northwest Mounted Police Chorus.

THE ALAN YOUNG SHOW (CBS) May 17, 1951.
Star: Alan Young. The Tom Mahoney Dancers.
    Guest Frances Langford sings "I Feel A Song Coming On" and "I Got Rhythm." Alan snarls up the long political career of a U.S. senator (Fred Clark). Alan and his wife are stymied in plans to attend a movie when a guest (Alan Hale Jr.) drops in.

PAUL WHITEMAN'S GOODYEAR REVUE (ABC) September 9, 1951.
Stars: Paul Whiteman and His Orchestra, Earl Wrightson, Maureen Cannon.
    First show of the season. Musical variety with guests Frances Langford and the Westbrook Dancers.

THE FRANCES LANGFORD-DON AMECHE SHOW (ABC)(Series) September 10, 1951 to March 14, 1952.
    Daytime variety.
    Cast

Stars	Frances Langford
	Don Ameche
Quizmaster	Neil Hamilton
Mrs. Fix-It	Fran Lee

"The Couple Next Door"	Jack Lemmon
	Cynthia Stone
Commercial Spokesperson	Angel
Orchestra	Tony Romano

Produced by Ward Byron.
Approx. 135 broadcasts.

THE COLGATE COMEDY HOUR (NBC) December 7, 1952.
Host: Bob Hope. Announcer: John Cannon. The Les Brown Orchestra.
Guests include Tony Martin, Frances Langford, and the 1953 *Esquire* magazine calendar girls. Bob, Tony, and Frances sing "A Fine Romance."

THE NAME'S THE SAME (ABC) March 10, 1953.
Host: Robert Q. Lewis. Panel: Joan Alexander, Meredith Willson, Jerry Lester. Announcer: John Reed King.
Singer Frances Langford drops in on the game wherein the celebrity panel must guess the names of contestants which match those of famous people or objects.

THE JACKIE GLEASON SHOW (CBS) "Honeymooners' Christmas Party" December 19, 1953.
Stars: Jackie Gleason, Art Carney, Audrey Meadows, Joyce Randolph. The June Taylor Dancers. Announcer: Jack Lescoulie. The Ray Bloch Orchestra.
Jackie's guests tonight are Frances Langford, Bert "Mad Russian" Gordon, and Eddie Hodges. It's Christmas Eve and Ralph Kramden (Jackie) has brought home the wrong potato salad. Alice (Meadows) sends him right back out and while he is gone, a parade of people drop in to cheer or raise havoc with the Kramdens and Nortons. Jackie also plays Joe the Bartender; the Poor Soul; Rudy the Repairman; and Reginald Van Gleason III.
Cop: Frank Marth.

Songs
Frances: "Great Day"; "I Love Paris."
Eddie: "Walking My Baby Back Home."

"FRANCES LANGFORD PRESENTS" (NBC)(Special) March 15, 1959.
Frances presides over an hour of variety. She shows films of herself, Bing Crosby, Fred Astaire, Jack Benny, and Betty Hutton entertaining

troops during World War II. Bob Hope performs for G.I.s in Alaska. A supermarket sketch with George Sanders and "Effie Klinker" (female dummy of Edgar Bergen). A hospital skit with "Charlie McCarthy" (dummy of Bergen), Julie London, and George. The David Rose Orchestra.

Songs

Frances: "Who Cares?"; "Speak Low"; "I'll Be Seeing You"; Just One Of Those Things"; "Au Revoir."
Hugh O'Brian, Frances: "Holiday For Horses."
Jerry Colonna: "I Love Life."
Frances, Tony Romano, Murray McEachern (trombone): "I Don't Want To Walk Without You"; "You're Priceless."
Julie: "Laura."
Julie, Bobby Troup: "Route 66."
The Four Freshmen: "Easy Street."
Julie, Four Freshmen: "Now, Baby, Now."
Julie, George: "Couple Of Average Joes."
All: "Let's Have A Party."

"THE BOB HOPE BUICK CHRISTMAS SHOW" (NBC)(Special)
January 13, 1960.

Bob entertained troops in Alaska this past Christmas (1959), and highlights of his tour are presented. A bear dances with Bob and Patty Thomas. A Japanese sketch with Bob, Steve McQueen, and Peter Leeds. A sketch called "Standing on the Corner" with the cast. The Skinnay Ennis Orchestra.

Songs

Frances Langford: "Night And Day"; "Silent Night."
Jayne Mansfield: "I've Got A Crush On You."
Bob, Jerry Colonna, Tony Romano: "If I Had My Way."
Neile Adams (McQueen's wife): "I Enjoy Being A Girl."

Variety: "Miss Langford still retains one of the top voices in the business, and was highly effective with her 'Night and Day' and in the ensemble songs."

"FRANCES LANGFORD PRESENTS" (NBC)(Special) May 1, 1960.

Frances gets her cast together for a flight to Hollywood to entertain the Movie Mothers Club. The show ends at the club, where the mothers of several Hollywood stars are introduced and serenaded by Frances and the gang. The Hermes Pan Dancers perform "Familiar Faces." The zany Three Stooges (Moe Howard, Larry Fine, Joe DeRita) in a hotel room sketch. A "Bickersons" skit with Frances and Don Ameche. Also, comedian Ken Murray, bongo drummer Jack Costanzo, and the Jud Conlon Singers. The Ray Heindorf Orchestra. *Broadcast in color.*

Songs
Frances: "My Mother's Eyes"; "Suppertime"; "Ave Maria."
All: "Old Rockin' Chair"; "High Noon"; "That's Amore"; "So In Love";
  "Que Sera Sera"; "I Won't Dance"; "I'm In The Mood For Love."
Frances, Johnny Mathis: "Skyliner."
Johnny: "Puttin' On The Ritz."
Mary Costa: "Sempre Libera"; "Holiday For Strings."
Bob [Robert] Cummings, Hermione Gingold: "I Remember It Well."

PERRY COMO'S KRAFT MUSIC HALL (NBC) March 15, 1961.
Star: Perry Como. Regulars: Renee Taylor, Bea Arthur, Milt Kamen. The Ray Charles Singers. The Peter Gennaro Dancers. Announcer: Frank Gallop. The Mitchell Ayres Orchestra.
      Guests Don Ameche and Frances Langford in a "Bickersons" skit. *Broadcast in color.*

Songs
Perry: "This New House"; "Too Young To Go Steady"; Hello, Young
      Lovers"; "Too Young."
Singers: "Commuter's Blues."

Ed Herlihy for Kraft Foods.

PERRY COMO'S KRAFT MUSIC HALL (NBC) May 17, 1961.
Star: Perry Como. Regulars: Renee Taylor, Bea Arthur, Milt Kamen. The Ray Charles Singers. The Peter Gennaro Dancers. Announcer: Frank Gallop. The Mitchell Ayres Orchestra.
      Don Ameche and Frances Langford return for another "Bickersons" skit. Also, the West Point Cadet Glee Club and comedian Paul Lynde. *Broadcast in color.*

Ed Herlihy for Kraft Foods.

THE DUPONT SHOW OF THE WEEK (NBC) "USO—Wherever They Go!" October 8, 1961.

The USO celebrates its 20th anniversary. The stars, under the auspices of the United Service Organization, have entertained and boosted the morale of our troops in both war and peacetime. Films of the various trips made by celebrities are shown. Frances Langford recalls her stint with Bob Hope, who is also on hand.

Jack Benny, Joe E. Brown, Eydie Gorme, Lena Horne, Danny Kaye, Steve Lawrence, Merle Oberon, Dick Powell, Debbie Reynolds, Danny Thomas, Harry S Truman, Dwight D. Eisenhower.

Archive footage of Ray Bolger, James Cagney, Gary Cooper, Bing Crosby, Marlene Dietrich, Leo Durocher, Kay Kyser, Marilyn Monroe, Martha Raye, Edward G. Robinson, Mickey Rooney, Jane Russell, Dinah Shore, Phil Silvers, Frank Sinatra.

Note: Beginning in the fall of 1966, all network programming is broadcast in color.

THE HOLLYWOOD PALACE (ABC) May 13, 1967.
Host: Bing Crosby. The Tom Hansen Dancers. Announcer: Dick Tufeld. The Mitchell Ayres Orchestra.

Don Ameche and Frances Langford re-create their famous radio portrayals of the battling "Bickersons." Bing and Frances rib Don about his 1939 movie role as Alexander Graham Bell. Also, the singing King Family; comic Louis Nye; singer Barbara McNair; comic pianist Yonely; and the Pollack Brothers trained elephants.

Songs
Bing: "Cockeyed Optimist."
Bing, Don, Frances: "All Alone By The Telephone."
Frances: "Call Me."
Barbara: "You're Gonna Hear From Me."
King Family: "Tradition."
King Sisters: "Watch What Happens."
Bing, Kings: "Bill Bailey."

THE JACKIE GLEASON SHOW (CBS) "The Match Game" November 29, 1969.
Stars: Jackie Gleason, Art Carney, Sheila MacRae, Jane Kean. The

June Taylor Dancers. Announcer: Johnny Olsen. The Sammy Spear Orchestra.

The Honeymooners breeze into the Windy City and meet Prof. Bonaventure Van Sickle (Frances Langford), the brain behind a computer-match service. Computer-wise, the Nortons' match really clicks—but Cupid somehow missed with the Kramdens! Who's at fault, man or machine? *Broadcast from Miami Beach, Florida.*

Songs
Frances: "Clyde."
Jackie: "I'm In Love All Over Again."

"BOB HOPE'S OVERSEAS CHRISTMAS TOURS: AROUND THE WORLD WITH THE TROOPS—1941-1972" (NBC)(Special) February 3, 10, 1980.

Bob Hope's three decades of entertaining American G.I.s is paid tribute in this two-part special. Included is never-seen footage culled from the armed forces and clips from previous specials.

Bob Hope, Anna Maria Alberghetti, Ursula Andress, Ann-Margret, Neil Armstrong, Fred Astaire, Carroll Baker, Lucille Ball, Johnny Bench, Vida Blue, Anita Bryant, James Cagney, Charo, Jerry Colonna, Vic Damone, Bette Davis, Jimmy Durante, Lola Falana, Henry Fonda, Redd Foxx, Zsa Zsa Gabor, Rosey [Roosevelt] Grier, Mickey Hargitay, Joey Heatherton, William Holden, Dolores Hope, Jack Jones, Randy Jones, Danny Kaye, Frances Langford, Gina Lollobrigida, Mickey Mantle, James Mason, Erin O'Brien, Janis Paige, Charley Pride, Dorothy Provine, Ginger Rogers, Alan Shepard, Dinah Shore, James Stewart, Lana Turner, Raquel Welch, Andy Williams.

Archive footage of Jack Benny, Humphrey Bogart, Bing Crosby, Marlene Dietrich, Clark Gable, Judy Garland, Betty Grable, Hedda Hopper, Al Jolson, Carole Lombard, Jayne Mansfield, Marilyn Monroe.

Song
Judy Garland: "Over The Rainbow" (Harold Arlen; E.Y. Harburg).

"STARS AND STRIPES: HOLLYWOOD AND WORLD WAR 2" (?) (Special) 1991.
Narrator: Tony Randall.

Documentary spotlighting the film capital's participation in the war effort.

Maxene Andrews, Eddie Bracken, Douglas Fairbanks Jr., Bob Hope, Anne Jeffreys, Shirley Jones, Dorothy Lamour, Frances Langford, Roddy McDowall, Debbie Reynolds, Cesar Romero, Sherwood Schwartz, Esther Williams.

"VICTORY IN THE PACIFIC" (CBS)(Special) August 3, 1995.
Co-Hosts: Dan Rather, H. Norman Schwarzkopf.

A look at the war in the Pacific (1941-45), including the stories of Japanese atrocities and the forced internment of Japanese-American citizens.

Eddie Albert, George [H.W.] Bush, Frances Langford, Patty Thomas. Archive footage of Greer Garson, Bob Hope.

BIOGRAPHY (A&E) "Don Ameche: Hollywood's Class Act" October 1, 1999.
Host: Peter Graves.

The life story of actor Don Ameche, star of radio, film, and television. Reminisces from family members Don Ameche Jr.; sister-in-law Rita Ameche; and niece Carol Ameche Nicholson. Also, film clips.

Ron Howard, John Landis, Frances Langford, Leonard Maltin, Fayard Nicholas.

SOURCES

The Animated Film Encyclopedia, A Complete Guide to American Shorts, Features, and Sequences, 1900-1979 by Graham Webb, McFarland, 2000.

The Animated Movie Guide by Jerry Beck, Chicago Review Press/A Cappella, 2005.

Archives of the Airwaves, 7 volumes, by Roger C. Paulson, BearManor Media, 2005-06.

The Big Broadcast, 1920-1950 by Frank Buxton and Bill Owen, Flare, 1973.

The Columbia Story by Clive Hirschhorn, Crown, 1989.

The Complete Directory to Prime Time Network and Cable TV Shows, 1946-Present, 9th Edition, by Tim Brooks and Earle Marsh, Ballantine, 2007.

Encyclopedia of American Radio, 1920-1960 by Luther F. Sies, McFarland, 2000.

The Encyclopedia of Daytime Television by Wesley Hyatt, Billboard/ Watson-Guptill, 1997.

Films in Review, "David Niven" by Anthony Thomas, February 1969, National Board of Review of Motion Pictures Inc.

Films in Review, "George Raft" by Jim Beaver, April 1978, National Board of Review of Motion Pictures Inc.

The Films of Ronald Reagan by Tony Thomas, Citadel Press, 1980.

Grand National, Producers Releasing Corporation, and Screen Guild/ Lippert: Complete Filmographies with Studio Histories by Ted Okuda, McFarland, 1989.

Halliwell's Film and Video Guide, 6th Edition, by Leslie Halliwell, Charles Scribner's Sons, 1987.

The Have Gun—Will Travel Companion by Martin Grams Jr. and Les Rayburn, OTR Publishing, 2000.

Hollywood Song, The Complete Film & Musical Companion, 3 volumes, by Ken Bloom, Facts on File, 1995.

The Honeymooners Lost Episodes, The Ralph, Alice, Ed and Trixie You've Waited 30 Years to See by Donna McCrohan and Peter Crescenti, Workman Publishing, 1986.

The I Love A Mystery Companion by Martin Grams Jr., OTR Publishing, 2003.

The Internet Movie Database, website @ www.imdb.com.

Jim Davidson's Classic TV Info, website @ www.classictvinfo.com

JJ's Radio Logs, website @ www.jjonz.us.

Leonard Maltin's Classic Movie Guide, edited by Leonard Maltin, et. al., Plume/Penguin, 2005.

Memories of Radio (catalog) by Dick Judge (self-published), 1980s.

The MGM Story by John Douglas Eames, Crown, 1982.

Movie Comedy Teams by Leonard Maltin, Signet/New American Library, 1970.

The New, Revised Ultimate History of Network Radio Programming and Guide to All Circulating Shows by Jay Hickerson, Presto Print II, 1996.

The Official Guide to the History of the Cavalcade of America Presented by DuPont by Martin Grams Jr., Morris Publishing, 1998.

On the Air: The Encyclopedia of Old-Time Radio by John Dunning, Oxford University Press, 1998.

The Paramount Story by John Douglas Eames, Crown, 1985.

Performers' Television Credits, 1948-2000, 3 volumes, by David M. Inman, McFarland, 2001.

Radio Drama, American Programs, 1932-1962 by Martin Grams Jr., McFarland, 2000.

RadioGOLDINdex, website @ www.radiogoldindex.com.

Radio Program Openings and Closings, 1931-1972 by Vincent Terrace, McFarland, 2003.

Radio's Golden Years, The Encyclopedia of Radio Programs 1930-1960 by Vincent Terrace, A.S. Barnes & Co., Inc., 1981.

Radio Speakers, Narrators, News Junkies, Sports Jockeys, Tattletales, Tipsters, Toastmasters and Coffee Klatch Couples Who Verbalized the Jargon of the Aural Ether from the 1920s to the 1980s—A Biographical Dictionary by Jim Cox, McFarland, 2007.

Radio Stars, An Illustrated Biographical Dictionary of 953 Performers, 1920 through 1960 by Thomas A. DeLong, McFarland, 1996.

The Railroad Hour, A History of the Radio Series by Gerald Wilson and Martin Grams Jr., BearManor Media, 2007.

The Republic Pictures Checklist by Len D. Martin, McFarland, 1998.

The RKO Story by Richard B. Jewell with Vernon Harbin, Arlington House, 1982.

Same Time...Same Station, An A-Z Guide to Radio from Jack Benny to Howard Stern by Ron Lackmann, Facts on File, 1996.

Songs By Sinatra: Radio, website @ www.songsbysinatra.com.

Sound Films, 1927-1939, a United States Filmography by Alan G. Fetrow, McFarland, 1992.

Spike Jones Off the Record, The Man Who Murdered Music by Jordan R. Young, Past Times Publishing, 1994.

Television Specials, 3,201 Entertainment Spectaculars, 1939-1993 by Vincent Terrace, McFarland, 1995.

Television Variety Shows by David M. Inman, McFarland, 2006.

Television Westerns Episode Guide, All United States Series, 1949-1996 by Harris M. Lentz III, McFarland, 1997.

39 Forever: Second Edition, Volume 1, by Laura Leff, BookSurge, 2004.

This Was Your Hit Parade by John R. Williams, Courier-Gazette Inc, 1973.

Tune In Yesterday, The Ultimate Encyclopedia of Old-Time Radio, 1925-1976 by John Dunning, Prentice-Hall, 1976.

TV Forecast, various issues 1949-52, edited by Robert A. Kubicek, Television Forecast Inc.

TV Guide, various issues 1950-69, edited by Walter Annenburg, et. al., Triangle Publications.

The United Artists Story by Ronald Bergan, Crown, 1986.

The Universal Story by Clive Hirschhorn, Crown, 1983.

Various radio logs by Ray Stanich, Randy Eidemiller, Jay Hickerson, Jerry Haendiges.

Vitaphone Films, A Catalogue of the Features and Shorts by Roy Liebman, McFarland, 2003.

The Warner Bros. Story by Clive Hirschhorn, Crown, 1979.

FRANCES LANGFORD SONGWRITING CREDITS

"Could You Spare a Dream?" (unpublished) March 11, 1938. Written with Carroll Kent Cooper

Lyrics for "It Was Music" (published by Forster Music Publisher). Words by Ralph Rose and FL, music by Ted Dreher. September 19, 1967

"Then You've Never Been Blue" from Every Night at Eight by Ted Fio Rito, Sam Lewis and Joe Young. Additional lyrics by FL. July 26, 1935

Index

Numbers in **bold** indicate photographs

Alan Young Show, The 316
Albert, Dora 123-124
All-American Co-Ed 38, 291
All-Star Thanksgiving Day Show 314
Ameche, Don 126, 161-164, **172**, 186, 187, 208-209, 210, 274, 275, 276, 278, 279, 316, 319, 320, 322
American Cancer Society Program 274
American Cruise 73, 266
Armed Forces V-J Program 273
Arnaz, Desi 37, 289
Arno, Peter 5, 313

Baker, Kenny 37-38, 264, 290
Ball, Lucille 37, **60**, 163, 289, 321
Ballew, Smith 37, **52, 54**, 284, 310
Bamboo Blonde, The 125-126, **127, 152, 153,** 165, 303-304
Beat the Band 164, **171**, 304-305
Benny, Jack 33, **136**, 183, 265, 268, 271, 276, 278, 280, 282, 317, 320, 321
Berkeley, Busby 34, 287
Berlin, Irving 122, 277, 297-298
Bickersons Fight Back, The 208
Bickersons Rematch, The 209
Bickersons, The 1, 161-164, 183-187, 208-210, 213, 274, 276, 279, 315, 319, 320
Bickersons, The (album) 208
Biography: Don Ameche: Hollywood's Class Act 322
Bob Hope's Overseas Christmas Tours 321

Bob Hope Buick Christmas Show, The 318
Born to Dance **15**, 34, 263, 285-286
Bracken, Eddie 37, 289, 322
Broadway Melody of 1936 33, **50**, 263, 282-283
"Broadway Rhythm" 33, 282, 311
Brown, Joe E. 183, 312, 320
Brown, Nacio Herb 33, 282, 311
Brown, Wally 122, 123, 301, 302
Bruce, Virginia **15**, 34, 285
Bush, Jeb 219, 229-230

Cagney, James 121, 123, 293, 294, 295, 320, 321
Camel Comedy Caravan 267
Cantor, Eddie 161, 264, 269, 273, 274, 276, 277
Career Girl 122, 300
Carney, Alan 122, 123, 301, 302
Cassino to Korea 183
Cavalcade of America, The 269, 271
Cavalcade of Stars 314, 315
Chase and Sanborn Program, The 273
Chase, Bill **18**
Chirstensen, Celia Langford 1, 3-4
Colgate Comedy Hour, The 193, 317
Colgate House Party, The 6, 262
Collegiate 33-34, 263, 283-284
Colonna, Bob 95
Colonna, Jerry 73, 74, 82, 87, 88, 94, 95, 96, **97, 98, 100, 101, 105, 107, 109, 110, 111, 117,** 124,

125, **134**, **136**, **144**, **151**, 265,
266, 267, 268, 269, 270, 271, 272,
273, 274, 275, 276, 280, 312, 318,
321
Combat America 295
"Come Down to New Orleans" 273
Command Performance 266, 267, 268,
269, 270, 271, 272, 274
Como, Perry 163, 213, 319
Cooper, Gary 34, 265, 312, 320
Cooper, Jerry **21**, 34, 287, 288
"Could You Spare a Dream?" 326
Cowboy in Manhattan 121, 297
Currier and Ives 164

Deputy Marshal 164-165, **182**, 306
Disney, Walt 164, 306
Dixie Jamboree 122-123, **137**, 300-
301
"Don't Believe Everything You Dream"
123, 302
Dorsey, Jimmy 37, 267
Dorsey, Tommy 36, 270, 275
Downs, Hugh 227-228
Dreaming Out Loud 37, 288-289
"Dreaming Out Loud" (song) 125, 289,
304
Drene Show, The 275
Drene Time 161-162
Duchin, Eddy 34, 286
Duffy's Tavern 278, 279
DuPont Show of the Week, The 320

"Easy to Love" 34, 285
Ebsen, Vilma 33, 282
Ebsen, Buddy **15**, 33, 282, 285
Ed Sullivan Show, The 262
Ed Wynn Show, The 315
Edwards, Ralph 302, 303, 304
Ellington, Duke 34, 286, 303
"Embraceable You" 80, 245, 255, 256
Ennis, Skinnay **70**, **144**, 273, 291, 296,
302, 312, 318
Entertaining the Troops 217-218
Every Night at Eight 33, **42**, 281-282,
326

Evinrude, Ralph 193-195, 196, 197,
198, **201**, **202**, **203**, **204**, **205**,
206, 207, 208, 213, 214, 215,
216, 217, **222**

Faye, Alice 33, 38, **42**, 281, 282
"Fine Romance, A" 193, 317
Fleischmann Hour, The 261
Follow the Band 122, 296
Forsythe, John **205**
Frances Langford and the News 265
Frances Langford Presents 207, 317-319
Frances Langford-Don Ameche Show,
The 187, 316-317
Frances Langford's Outrigger Resort
196, 213-216, **222**, **225**
Frank Morgan Show, The 263
Freed, Arthur 33, 282, 310, 311
Frigidaire Comedy Hour: Michael Todd
's Revue 315

Garland, Judy 73, 265, 271, 272, 274,
285, 308, 321
George Burns and Gracie Allen Show,
The 263
George White's Scandals 6, 165
Girl Rush 122, 301-302
Gleason, Jackie 163, 193, 315, 317, 320
Glenn Miller Story, The 193, 307-309
Goodman, Benny 34, 262, 287, 315
Gordon, Mack 34, 283, 284, 308
Gould, Dave 33, 283, 286, 309
Grable, Betty 38, 283, 310, 321
"Great Day" 193, 317
Greek War Relief Fund 265
Guest Star 278
Gulf Screen Guild Theatre, The 265

Haddad, Karan 199
Hall, Jon 34-37, **39**, **40**, **42**, **61**, **62**, 78,
164-165, **182**, 183, 187, **190**,
191, 193, 264, 277, 278, 306,
311, 316
Have Gun – Will Travel 279
"Having a Good Time, Wish You Were
Here" 37

Hedda Hopper's Hollywood No. 4 312
Here Goes the Bride 5, 313
Here's to Veterans 274, 276
"Hideout in Hidden Valley" 165, 306
Himber, Richard 6, 262
Hit Parade of 1941, The 37-38, 290
Hit Parade, The 34, 38, 286-287
Hollywood Hotel (radio) 5, **21**, 34, 36, 263
Hollywood Hotel (movie) 5, 34, 287-288
Hollywood Palace, The 320
Hope, Bob 73-96, **76, 77, 97, 98, 100,**
    101, 103, 105, 106, 107, 109,
    110, 111, 117, 123, 124, 125,
    134, 136, 139, 144, 151, 159,
    161, 162, 183, 187, **189,** 193,
    207-208, 218, 221, **225,** 228, 229,
    230, 265, 266, 267, 268, 269, 270,
    271, 272, 273, 274, 276, 278, 280,
    295, 312, 317, 318, 320, 321, 322
Hope, Dolores 218, **223,** 321
Hopper, Hedda 207, 312, 321
Howard, Shemp 121, 292
Hurricane Island 183
Husband and Wife 207

"I Can't Believe It's True" 37
"I Couldn't Sleep a Wink Last Night"
    123, 302, 304
"I Don't Want to Make History" 37, 284
"I Feel a Song Coming On" 264, 281,
    316
"I Got Rhythm" 316
"I Love Paris" 193, 317
I Never Left Home 272
"I'm in Love" 164, 304
"I'm in the Mood for Love" 33, 73, 195,
    198, 218, 281, 284, 303, 319
"I've Got My Fingers Crossed" 164, 304
"I've Got You Under My Skin" 34, 285
"It Was Music" 326
"It's Been a Long, Long Time" 274

Jack Benny Program, The 38, **136**
Jack Carter Show, The 314, 316
Jackie Gleason Show, The 193, 317, 320-
    321

Langford, James 5, 73, 214
Joan Davis Show, The 277

Katzman, Sam 165, 183, 307
Kaye, Danny 161, 271, 277, 320, 321
Kelly, Patsy 33, **42,** 281, 282, 290
Ken Murray Show, The 316
King, Larry 221
"Kissin' Well" 164, 304
Knight's Orchestra 262
Kraft Music Hall 264, 319
Krupa, Gene 164, **171,** 287, 304, 307

Landi, Linda 123
Last Train from Bombay 165
Lawrence, Ed 215-216, **222**
Leo Forbstein Memorial Special 277
"Let That Be a Lesson to You" 34, 287
Let's Keep Going: USO Camp Shows 278
"Levis, Plaid Shirt and Spurs" 165, 306
Linkletter, Art 123, **205,** 274, 303
Lucky Strike Hit Parade, The 263
Lum and Abner 37, 262, 275, 279
Lux Radio Theatre, The 272

Make Mine Laughs 165
March of Dimes Special 269
Martin and Lewis Show, The 278
Maxwell House Coffee Time 274, 275-
    276
Melody Kaleidoscope 261
Melody Time 164, 305-306
Memo for Joe 312
Merkel, Una **15,** 282, 285, 297
Merrick, Mahlon 33, 306
MGM Syndicated Air Trailers 263
Miller, Ann 37, 289, 290
Mississippi Gambler 121, **129,** 292-293
Mitchum, Robert 122, 296, 301
Modernaires, The 193, 307, 308
"Moonlight Over the Islands" 165, 304
Murray, Ken 37, 38, 291, 316, 319
Music for Millions 271
Musical Americana 265
*My America: What My Country Means
    to Me* 227-229

"My Blue Heaven" 122, 299
"My Melancholy Baby" 122, 292, 296

Name's the Same, The 193, 317
Nathan, George Jean 5-6, 34, 78
National Mobilization for Human Needs 264
Never a Dull Moment 122, **132**, 299
"Night and Day" 5, 80, 318
Norris, Edward 36, 122, 300, 311
"Now's the Time to Buy a Bond" 271

Old Gold Show, The 276
"Once Upon a Wintertime" 164, 305
"Over There" 121, 293
Paige, Robert 121, 297
Palm Springs (1936) 37, **51**, **52**, **53**, **54**, 263, 284-285
Parade of Music, A 279
Parker, Frank 34
Parker, Lew 1, 163, 183, 184, 186, 279, 315
Parsons, Louella 5, 34, 263, 287
Paul Whiteman's Goodyear Revue 316
Penner, Joe 33-34, 283
People Are Funny 123, 303
"People Will Say We're In Love" 267
Pepsodent Show, The **134**, 265, 266, 267, 268, 269, 270, 273, 276
Picture People No. 10: Hollywood At Home 311-312
Picture People No. 4: Stars Day Off 311
"Please Don't Cry" 269
Plough's Musical Courier 6
Porter, Cole 5, 34, 265, 285
Powell, Dick 5, 34, 73, 263, 265, 266, 287, 288, 320
Powell, Eleanor **15**, 33, 282, 285
Pure in Heart, The 5, 313-314
Purple Heart Diary (1951) 187, 307
"Purple Heart Diary" (column) 166-170, 187, 233-259
Purple Heart Theatre, The 275

Quillan, Eddie 122, 123, 296, 300

Radio Hall of Fame, The 272
Radio Stars on Parade 123, 302
Raft, George 33, 281
Railroad Hour, The 278
Rambling 'Round Radio Row #2 310
Rapp, Philip 1, 161-162, 208-210
Raye, Martha 208, 268, 320
Recollections at Thirty 279
Red Feather Preview 278
Regan, Phil 34, 286, 314
Remember Me When I Am Gone 221
Request Performance 273, 274
Revel, Harry 34, 283, 284, 302
Ritz Brothers, The 122, **132**, 299, 314
Roach, Hal 38, 291
"Rocking in the Rocket Room" 207
Rodgers & Hart 37, 289, 294
Rogers, Ginger 207, 321
Roll Call 277
Romano, Tony 1, 73-75, **77**, 82, 89, 94, 96, **106**, **149**, **175**, **178**, 187, **192**, 207, 218, 268, 271, 273, 279, 280, 295, 300, 302, 307, 312, 317, 318
Rose, David 207, 299, 318
Royal Gelatin Hour, The 264
Rudy Vallee Alumni Reunion 264

Sailor's Holiday 123
Salute to Bob Hope, A 280
"Saving Myself for Bill" 267
Screen Snapshots Series 25, No. 7 312-313
Seventh War Loan Drive, The 272
"Shoo Shoo, Baby" 269
"Silhouetted in the Moonlight" 34, 287
Silvers, Sid **15**, 282, 285
"Sleepy Time Gal" 122, 299
Smith, Nancy 220
Soldiers in Greasepaint 268
Songs by Sinatra 273
Southern Cruise 265-266
Spartan Hour, The 262
"Speaking Confidentially" 33, 281
Stafford, Hanley 38, 291
Stage Door Canteen 272
Stanton, Kim 95, 195-196, 218, 219

Star of the Family 315-316
Star Time 183-186, 315
Stars and Stripes: Hollywood and World War 2 321-322
Stars on Parade 279
Stars Over Hollywood 266
Stewart, James **15**, 34, 285, 307, 309, 321
Stuart, Harold 218-219, **225**, **226**
Studebaker Program, The 6
Subway Symphony, The 309-310
Sullivan, Ed 5, 262
Sunkist Stars at Palm Springs 310-311
Swing It Soldier 38, **70**, 291-292
"Swing Low, Sweet Rhythm" 38, 290
"Swingin' the Jinx Away" 34, 285, 286
Swingtime 280
Symphonies Under the Stars 277

Taylor, Kent 121, 292
Taylor, Robert 33, 282
Terry, Phillp **118**, **171**, 304
Tex and Jinx Show 277
Texaco Star Theatre, The 37, 264
"That Old Black Magic" 80, 302
"Then You've Never Been Blue" 33, 281, 326
"There Goes That Song Again" 272
This is New York 279
This Is the Army 122, 297-299
Thomas, Danny 163, 274, 276, 320
Thomas, Patty **98**, **100**, **102**, **108**, 124, **128**, **148**, 207, 217, 218, 221, 235, 238, 254, 318, 322
Too Many Girls 37, **60**, **72**, 289-290
Treasury Star Parade 267
Truman, President Harry S 165-167, 170, 218, 273, 320
Truth or Consequences 123
U.S.O. Farewell Program 276

V-E Day Special, The 272
Vallee, Rudy 4-5, 123, 261, 264, 303
Victory Chest Program, The 273
Victory in the Pacific 322

Wade, Russell **127**, 303
Walter Wanger's Vogues of 1938 34
Wanger, Walter 5, 34, 282, 285
War Telescope 267
"What Does He Look Like?" 122, 298
"When You Speak with Your Eyes" 207
Which is Which? 271
"Who Am I?" 38, 283, 290
Wick, Charles Z. 195, 207
Wilson, Don 38, 275, 282, 291, 302
Winchell, Walter 34
Witt, Eli 5

Yankee Doodle Dandy 121, 293-295
"You Are My Lucky Star" 33, 282, 311
"You Hit the Spot" 34, 283
"You Made Me Love You" 93
"You Turned the Tables on Me" 263
"Young and Healthy" 262
Young, Victor 37, 271, 284, 307
Your All-Time Hit Parade 270
Your Hit Parade 266

Lightning Source UK Ltd.
Milton Keynes UK
UKHW021151220819
348364UK00010B/2099/P